Lao Folktales

World Folklore Advisory Board

Lao Folktales

Wajuppa Tossa, with Kongdeuane Nettavong

Edited by Margaret Read MacDonald

World Folklore Series

LIBRARIES
UNLIMITED

A Member of the Greenwood Publishing Group

Westport, Connecticut • London

Library of Congress Cataloging-in-Publication Data

Wayupha Thotsa.
  Lao folktales / Wajuppa Tossa with Kongdeuane Nettavong ; edited by Margaret Read MacDonald.
  p. cm. — (World folklore series)
  Includes bibliographical references and index.
  ISBN 978-1-59158-345-5 (alk. paper)
  1. Tales—Laos. 2. Laos—Folklore. I. Kongduan Nettavong. II. MacDonald, Margaret Read,
  1940- III. Title.
  GR311.W39 2008
  398.209594—dc22   2007040340

British Library Cataloguing in Publication Data is available.

Library of Congress Catalog Card Number: 2007040340
ISBN: 978–1–59158–345–5

First published in 2008

Libraries Unlimited, 88 Post Road West, Westport, CT 06881
A Member of the Greenwood Publishing Group, Inc.
www.lu.com

Printed in the United States of America

The paper used in this book complies with the
Permanent Paper Standard issued by the National
Information Standards Organization (Z39.48–1984).

10 9 8 7 6 5 4 3 2 1

The publisher has done its best to make sure the instructions and/or recipes in this book are correct.
However, users should apply judgment and experience when preparing recipes, especially parents
and teachers working with young people. The publisher accepts no responsibility for the outcome of
any recipe included in this volume.

CONTENTS

Part 1: Lao Folktales

Part 2: Buddhist *Jataka* and Moral Tales

Part 3: Tales of Xiang Miang and Other Tricksters

Part 4: Tales of Fools

Part 5: Animal Tales

Part 6: Riddle Tales

Part 7: Ghost Stories

Part 8: Tales of Magic and Elaborate Tales

Part 9: Tales of Helpful Gods and Spirits

Part 10: Place Legends

Part 11: Origin Myths of the Lao People

Part 12: Folk Epics

Part 13: Lao Food, Crafts, and Games

ACKNOWLEDGMENTS

I would like first of all to thank Dr. Margaret Read MacDonald for her understanding of the importance of Lao folktales. It has been a great privilege to have her as the editor and mentor for this project. My thanks must also go to the supervisors of the Lao folklore course online project of the Center for Southeast Asian Studies: Dr. John Hartmann, Dr. George Henry, Dr. Robert Zerwekh, and Dr. Susan Russell. And my thanks for the administrative assistance of Ms. Julie Lamb, outreach coordinator of the center. It was there that the collection of Lao folktales began to take shape. I am indebted to Mr. Art Crisfield for introducing me to Ajan Kongdeuane Nettavong, director of the Lao National Library, who in turn introduced me to more Lao scholars and traditional storytellers. Ms. Sivilay Sopha, assistant to Ajan Kongdeuane at the time, was helpful in seeking storytellers' residences for the interviews as well as sharing her own folktales for the collection. I would like to thank Mme. Dala Viravong Kalaya, Mr. Outhine Bounyavong, and Mrs. Doungdeuane Viravong Bounyavong, who were among the first group of people I met before the beginning of any project in Laos, and they introduced me to many important literary preservation projects in Laos.

When we started this book, I had a chance to work with administrators of organizations in Laos. I greatly appreciate the information they provided and their generous assistance. Thanks to Mr. Sombath Somphone, director of Participatory Development Training Center (PADETC); Ms. Bouchanh Thanouvong, head of Education Affairs at PADETC; Mr. Souban Luanglahd, director of Lao Children's Cultural Center, and his staff; and Mme. Xuyen Dangers, director of Donkoi Children's Development Center. Through these people I met more storytellers, including Elder Bounyok Saensounthone; Mr. Khamsing Vongsavang; Ms. Chanpheng Singphet; Ms. Duangkhay Luangphasi; and the Buddhist monks like Pha Sounantha Theeraphanyo, Pha Viengsamay, Pha Soubandit Duangvongsa, and Pha Xaysomphone Phithivan. In the process of writing the book in the United States during spring 2006, the collected information was not always clear to me. Ms. Phanida Phunkrathok and Ms. Wantana Khotephuwiang, two of my former students, volunteered to travel to Vientiane to search for clarification. I am thankful to them as well.

I am grateful to the following storytellers in Isaan, who either retold stories to me directly or contributed their stories in the storytelling classes, camps, workshops, and festivals held in Mahasarakham: Phra Inta Kaweewong from Wat Sa-ahdsomboon, Roi-Et, Natthakan Photjanaphimon, Kunthari Saichua, Manatchanok Thongkanok, Suched Somsa,

Suphaphit Khantha, Khambao Thaenna, and Somboon Thana-uoan. I also learned about many folktales from the late abbot of Mahachai Temple in Mahasarakham, Phra Ariyanuwat, and from the late Mr. Jinda Duangjai, who left valuable resources for the study of Lao folk literature in print via Khlang Nanatham Publishing House in Khonkaen.

I would like to thank Mr. Prasong Saihong, Mr. Gerald Fierst, and Mrs. Suwannee Girdchuen for supplying many photographs for the book. While I was editing the final manuscript in the United States, Ms. JonLee Joseph, in Mahasarakhsm, helped by taking care of my house and my grandmother. I greatly appreciate her friendship and moral support for my work.

Finally, I would like to thank my parents and grandparents, who told me many wondrous stories when I was young. Without them, I would not have a love of and attachment to the folktales of the Lao people from both sides of the Mekong River.

Wajuppa Tossa

My thanks go to Dr. Wajuppa Tossa and Dr. Margaret Read MacDonald for their genuine love of Lao folktales and for including me in the project. I am indebted to many Lao scholars, who generously gave me both stories and information about the Lao people and culture, including Than Kidaeng Phonekasemsouk and Elder Bounyok Saensounthone. My thanks must also go to my able assistants, Sivilay Sopha, Khanthamalee Yangnouvong, and Saengjan Phameuang.

Note on spelling in this book: For the names of Lao scholars, I used the original English spellings given to me. For the Lao storytellers whose names were given to me in Lao, I tried to use the same system that Lao scholars use. For the Isaan names and Lao words that appeared in the stories, I tried to use the romanization system from the Library of Congress's *Romanization of Lao and Thai Languages* to avoid mispronunciation. For example, the word "fire" is the same in Isaan and Lao: *fi,* pronounced as in the term "hi fi." In the Lao romanization, it may be *"fay,"* and the vowel sound /ay/ should be pronounced like the word /fi/. But to general English speakers, the romanization would easily be pronounced like a person's name, "Fay," which does not mean "fire."

Kongdeuane Nettavong

AN INTRODUCTION TO OUR AUTHORS

The stories in this book reach us through a long path. Somewhere in Laos or Isaan—the Lao culture area of Northeastern Thailand—someone once told these stories. Some were heard by our authors directly from the tellers and passed on in this book. Others were heard by monks, teachers, or other folktale collectors and written down. These were then read by our authors and retold. We have given the names and home places of the original tellers when possible. But the voices of our two author-retellers are authentic ones. Both grew up hearing stories told. Both are very much a part of the Lao folk culture from which these stories grow. Both now work with language and books and desire to preserve these stories for a wider audience. Kongdeuane is the director of the Lao National Library in Laos, and Wajuppa is an associate professor of English and American literature at Mahasarakham University in Northeastern Thailand, or Isaan.

Kongdeuane Nettavong has heard stories since her childhood. She is of the Lao Phuan people and grew up in Xiang Khouang. Some of the stories retold here are from her own memory. Some are from other tellers, especially tales collected by the scholar Mr. Kidaeng Phonekasemsouk.

Dr. Wajuppa Tossa grew up in That Phanom, a small town on the Thai side of the Mekong River. She is of the Lao culture, but by the time she was born her area was a part of Thailand. So the Thai language was imposed in school and government. She tells me that at one time the Thai government issued an order that only Thai was to be spoken from then on. No ancient palm leaf manuscripts could be used in schools. Some older people misunderstood this to mean that no Lao texts would be allowed to exist. Some families burned their old palm leaf manuscripts, which contained the ancient stories. These were written in the old Lao language, and the people feared they would be punished if the manuscripts were found in their homes. Others, fortunately, took their palm leaf manuscripts to the temple, where they were preserved. Today caches of these old manuscripts still exist in temples throughout Isaan.

Dr. Wajuppa translated one of the Lao epics, *Phadaeng Nang Ai,* into English as her Ph.D. dissertation at Drew University. A former monk, Phra Ariyanuwat Khemajari from Mahachai Temple in Mahasarakham, had translated the ancient Lao language palm leaf manuscript into contemporary Lao, using the Thai alphabet, and Dr. Wajuppa made her

English translation from this. Her text attempts to show the amazing internal rhyme pattern of the Lao epic, which rhymes at three places within each line and between the first and second lines. She uses the old Lao poetry format of splitting the two lines into four-eight sections in her English translation.

As a professor at Mahasarakham University, Dr. Wajuppa became increasingly concerned about the lack of Lao culture in Isaan. She devised a plan to increase pride in the local language through storytelling. From 1995 to the present day, Wajuppa has taught storytelling courses and collected folktales in Isaan. She has taught many young teachers storytelling techniques and has retold numerous Lao folktales for use in the classroom.

I was fortunate to spend some months working with Dr. Wajuppa in Mahasarakham in 1995–1997. I was invited as a Fulbright Scholar to help jump-start her storytelling project. Our work together has continued through the years on numerous storytelling and folklore endeavors. I met Kongdeuane on a storytelling tour of Laos in 2006. Dr. Wajuppa has been working with Kongdeuane since 2001 on various storytelling projects in Laos.

In 2001 Dr. Wajuppa and Prasong Saihong went to the Center for Southeast Asian Studies at Northern Illinois University to create a Lao folklore course for their Web site, www.seasite.niu.edu/lao/folklore. They had worked with Kongdeuane to collect published tales in the Lao language and tales from interviews with local storytellers in Vientiane. The administrators of the Web site give permission for materials placed on the site to be used in this book.

Wajuppa's most recent project is collecting folktales from traditional tellers in villages in Laos and Isaan. She is also interviewing the tellers to record information about their lives and their use of story in their communities. In this work she has the support of Mahasarakham University and The Participatory Development Training Center (PADETC) of Vientiane, Laos. The work is difficult because travel to some of the remote mountainous areas of Laos is dangerous at times, and the government periodically closes travel to residents of other countries.

I am proud to be able to bring the work of these fine scholars to our readers. They have worked incessantly to preserve the folklore of their culture, and it is wonderful that they have taken time to provide this small glimpse into Lao folklore for English readers to enjoy.

Margaret Read MacDonald, Editor
Guemes Island, Washington, August 2007

MAP OF LAOS

PART 1

Lao Folktales

*T*he stories in this book are told by the Lao people. Those people do not live just in the country of Laos, and not all of the people who live in Laos are ethnic Lao. Instead, there is a Lao culture area that includes the lowland areas of Laos bordering the Mekong River and the part of Thailand bordering the Mekong River in the provinces south of Nong Khai and Vientiane. This area of Thailand is called, Isaan, or Northeastern Thailand. Because the political boundaries have been drawn in such a way that Northeastern Thailand is part of the country of Thailand, the fact that most of the people living there are ethnically Lao is sometimes overlooked.

Lao on both sides of the Mekong speak the Lao language, with slight dialectical differences according to region. The Lao living in Thailand also speak Thai, but some of the Lao in Thailand are losing facility with their own Lao language because the media, education, and government are all provided only in Bangkok Thai.

The Lao people on both sides of the Mekong share a love for special delicacies such as *laab* (salad made from diced meat or fish and vegetables) and *pla dek* (sauce made from fermented fish paste). The rice eaten here is mostly sticky rice. This is glutinous rice that is steamed, then rolled into little balls to dip into the various sauces and meat and vegetable dishes. Specially woven sticky rice baskets are used to carry the cooked rice.

The rice has traditionally been grown with the aid of water buffalo, which pull the plows. The water buffalo has been an important part of rural life. Young boys take the buffalo to the river to cool off during the heat of the day and take care of them. At night the buffalo are brought home and sleep under the houses. The houses are raised on poles, which allows cool air to circulate and also provides a pleasant place for people and animals to rest out of the sun and rain.

The Lao women are noted for their fine weaving of both silk and cotton cloth. They are expert at a weaving technique called *ikat,* in which the threads are dyed before being put onto the loom. This requires extraordinary skill in the dying process and care in matching the threads up exactly according to the design during the weaving.

The Lao are a Buddhist people, and you will read much in these stories about monks and novices. Young boys may go to the *wat* (temple) and stay for a few weeks to learn Buddhist precepts. During this time they will take vows, have their heads shaved, and wear the robes of a novice. At one time the *wat* was where most boys were trained in reading and writing. But today both boys and girls attend public schools, though some orphaned or poor boys may be raised by monks at the *wat*. The Buddha was a wise teacher in India whose followers spread word of his teachings throughout Asia. Buddhist precepts require kindness to all creatures, both human and animal. The five rules of conduct for laypeople are (1) do not kill any living thing, (2) do not steal, (3) do not act unchastely, (4) do not lie, and (5) do not drink intoxicating beverages. There are also three treasures of Buddhism: the Lord Buddha; the Dharma, or teachings; and the Sanghka, or brotherhood of monks. Lao people respect these.

In addition to their Buddhist religion, the Lao have an extensive cosmology of mystical beings, which are elaborated in their own mythology. Some of this is given in Parts 11 and 12. This mythology is known by most Lao people and is an important component of their cultural life.

I hope you enjoy the stories in this book. The Lao are a fun-loving people with a great sense of humor. It shows up in these stories, as does their incredible imagination!

Margaret Read MacDonald, Editor

GENERAL INFORMATION ABOUT LAO GEOGRAPHY, HISTORY, AND PEOPLES

Kongdeuane Nettavong, librarian at the National Library in Vientiane

Lao Geography and Climate

Laos as a nation-state presently occupies approximately 91,425 square miles in Southeast Asia. To the north are Myanmar (Burma) and China. Vietnam spreads along the eastern and part of the southern borders of Laos. Kampuchea (Cambodia) is also a neighboring country to the south. To the west, the Mekong River forms the border between Laos and Thailand. Along the Mekong River's banks are the major cities of Laos: the ancient capital, Luang Phabang, in the north; the present-day capital, Vientiane, in the center; and Sawannakhet and Champasak in the south. Geographically, Laos covers three major settings: the mountainous lands, called *Lao Suung* (Highland Laos); the valley area in the lower north, called *Lao Thoeng* (Northern Laos); and the area along the Mekong River, called *Lao Lum* (Lowland Laos).

Like most countries in Southeast Asia, Laos enjoys the tropical climate of three seasons: the rainy season between May and September; the cool season between October and February; and the summer, between March and May. Temperatures vary according to location. In highland Laos, during the cool season the temperature can drop as low as 50 degrees Fahrenheit. In lowland Laos the temperature in the summer can rise to as much as 104 degrees Fahrenheit. During the rainy season the weather is cooler, with periods of heavy rainfall.

Brief History

The Lao people have occupied this land for a long time. The early Lao people confronted all kinds of dangers and hardships to establish the country in which the Lao now live, the Lao People's Democratic Republic. There may have been people living in the Lao area in the Palaeolithic (500,000–20,000 B.C.), Mesolithic (20,000–8,000 B.C.), and Neolithic (8,000–6,000 B.C.) ages. Lao society established a hierachical structure, with tribes

---

and clans spread all over the land, sometime between 6,000 and 1200 B.C. During this period each tribe or group lived autonomously, in various settings.

Between 1200 B.C and the twelfth century A.D. the centers of administration declined in number, as many tribes consolidated power and founded autonomous cities. These cities—particularly those along the Mekong River from north to south, including Suwannakhomkham, Xiang Saen, Xiang Dong, Xiang Thong, Vientiane, Na Hong, Xiang Sa, Sikhottabong, Champasak, and other other cities in the east, such as Sipsong Panna and Sipsong Cuthai—enjoyed close relationships. There were also cities along tributaries of the Mekong River such as the Mun River and Chee River.

Lao cities were consolidated into one kingdom, called Lan Xang, in A.D. 1353, under the leadership of Phaya Fa-ngum. According to ancient Lao chronicles such as *Khun Bulom* and *Urangkhathat*, Lao civilization and culture grew along the central Mekong River between the twelfth and nineteenth centuries.

The Lan Xang Kingdom comprised many tribes, which lived off the fertile land along the Mekong River, where they could find abundant plants and animals. The Mekong River was an important transportation route for the various tribes. Over time the tribes formed their own unique cultures with their own languages, writing, foods, costumes, festivals, rites, religion, and manners. However, the tribes were also part of the mainstream culture, under which they lived together peacefully. There were no major conflicts between the tribes during the period of the Lan Xang Kingdom. Most conflicts were with external feudal powers. Because of the self-sufficient economy of this agricultural region, Laos at that period can be said to have been undeveloped. The Lao way of life depended entirely on natural resources. However, the cooperation among tribes made it possible for the kingdom of Lan Xang to become very powerful, with its capital at Xiang Khwang. Lan Xang was one of the most stable polities in terms of politics, Buddhism, and culture. The kingdom reached its greatest height of development during this period.

After a number of kings had reigned, the capital was moved to Luang Phabang. Between 1548 and 1571, Phacao Xaiyaset moved the capital to Vientiane. He built important temples such as Pha That Luang and the temple where the Emerald Buddha Image first resided.

During the reign of Phachao Suriyawongsathammathirat (1638–1695), Laos became involved in diplomatic relationships with foreign merchants from Holland (the Dutch East India Company) and missionaries from Italy. Chronicles written by these foreign visitors described the beauty of Vientiane, which they considered the most beautiful capital in Southeast Asia. They found the Lao rites, culture, and customs interesting and the land rich with plants and animals.

However, the Lan Xang Kingdom fell into deep trouble because of foreign invasions and internal conflicts. Consequently, Lan Xang was split into three kingdoms—Champasak, Luang Phabang, and Vientiane—which weakened it and left it open to invasion by a neighboring feudal power, Siam, in 1779. In 1893 Laos became a colony of France, with resulting loss of land and freedom. In 1975 Laos became an independent country, doing away with feudalism, and established itself as the Lao People's Democratic Republic.

The Lao People and Their Ways of Life

Because of its diverse geographic settings, Laos is a land rich with the cultural heritage of various ethnic groups. Among the 6,368,481 people in Laos (July 2006 est.; http://www.cia.gov/cia/publications/factbook/geos/la.html#Geo) are forty-nine ethnic groups, scattered in various areas of Laos in four linguistic families. These ethnic groups can be classified in three major categories: Lao Loum (lowland), 70 percent; Lao Theung (upland), 20 percent; and Lao Soung (highland), including the Hmong and the Yao, approximately 10 percent. Some 1 percent of the population is Vietnamese or Chinese.

Lao Loum (lowland) speak languages in the Lao-Tai family. They live in the lowland areas near big rivers in eighteen provinces, with one special zone called Xaisomboun. Most are Buddhists. They depend on agriculture, especially growing rice. They tend to live in groups in big cities without mixing with other tribes. Some make a living by selling merchandise, both through private enterprise and through government affiliation. The lowland Lao-Tai generally consume glutinous rice. Some lowland Lao are fishermen along the Mekong River and other rivers. They fish during the high fishing season. The main staples of their diet are fish and crabs. They preserve the fish for consumption during the low fishing season or the rice planting season and make salted fish called *paa daeg*. They have a saying, "Rice field Lao eat *paa daeg,* salted and pickled fish."

The upper lowland ethnic groups, such as the *Tai Phuan, Tai Dam,* and *Tai Daeng,* have their own ways of preserving fish for consumption throughout the entire year, such as pickling, fermenting, and drying. The lowlanders also enjoy the meat of animals they raise for sale and consumption, such as cows, buffalo, chickens, and ducks. Food preparation varies from tribe to tribe. The *Tai Phuan,* one of the largest ethnic groups, living in Xiangkhoang district along the Nguem River and in Vientiane, tend to eat salted fish and salted swallows, soy bean paste, dry soy bean curds, stewed bamboo shoots, pickled bamboo shoots, and chili peppers (red, green, fresh, and dried). The *Tai Daeng, Tai Dam,* and *Tai Neua* enjoy soy beans made into paste, salted soy beans, and fish.

The southern lowland Lao people, from Sawannakhet down to Champasak, eat food raw or medium raw, such as the meat salads called *laab* and *koi.* They also eat raw salted and pickled fish (small fish called *pa soi).* A traditional local vegetable stew with various spices is also popular in Laos.

Lao people's clothes are exquisite. The art of weaving has been passed on from generation to generation. Tai-Lao speaking groups are well known for their elaborate weaving designs. The Lao like to wear clothes made from their own handmade cloth. Women are known to be great cloth weavers, while men tend to be skilled in weaving baskets for household use and for sale. The men's products include mats, baskets, glutinous rice steamers and boxes, food trays, silkworm trays, and fishing nets, to name a few. Some men are skilled in pottery making, black smithing, and painting designs on candles, wood, temple walls, and roofs. The men are also good at making musical instruments such as *khaen* (wind instruments made of bamboo pipes), flutes, *saws* (stringed instruments), and *lanads* (xylophone-like instruments).

Among the lowland Lao is a distinctive and unified group of people called *Phu Tai*, who live from Khammoun province down to Sawannakhet. This group of people is well known for their art of dyeing cloth using natural pigments. They plant cotton and weave cotton cloth. Their most distinctive dish is *nam khisut*, a black sauce made of boiled pickled vegetables. It is eaten with every meal.

Lao Theung (upland) Lao live in the high plains and valleys. Their languages are among the Mon-Khmer language family. Some of them believe in animism and ancestral spirits, guardian spirits of the village and of the forest, while others have converted to Buddhism and Christianity. They live off their farms and gardens, planting rice, fruit, and vegetables. They are good at hunting animals in the forest as well as gathering forest foods and herbs. There are many tribes within this group, each with a different way of life. In the north are the *Khamu* (*Khammu*). In the central and southern parts of Laos are the *Bid, Brao, Harak, Idou, Kabkae, Katang, Katou, Khmer, Khmu, Khom, Kri, Krieng, Lamed, Lavy, Makong, Meuang, Ngouane, Oi, Pray, Samtao, Singmou, Souai, Ta-oi, Thene, Toum, Trieng, Try, Yeh,* and *Yrou.*

The Lao Theung have extraordinary weaving skills, particularly the cloths used as belts, and their basketry is much admired by visitors. They are also skilled in hunting wild animals in the forest. Their diet depends on what they can find in nature, not from planting. Their rice farming does not yield good crops, so they plant root vegetables such as taro and yams. Their main food source is roots dug up in the forest, where they spend most of their time. They are diligent people, going to bed late and getting up early every day and traveling far in the forest. Both men and women work hard, the women clearing the fields, finding water and firewood, preparing rice, and raising children. The Lao Theung are known for being honest and sincere. The upland Lao eat meat from small animals such as rats and squirrels, which they trap and dry for later consumption. They eat spicy food made with salt and chili peppers, but do not eat pickled or salted fish. They raise large animals like cows and buffalo, which they will eat only during special festivals in the village. The upland Lao in many areas have intermarried with the lowland Lao.

The last group of Lao people are the Lao Soung (the highland), whose languages are in the Tibeto-Burmese, Chinese, and Hmong-Ioumein families. They live in the high mountains where the weather is cool. The highlanders include the Ahka, Hayi, Hor, Lahou, Lolo, Sila, and Singsali. The Hmong-Ioumen language family has two main groupings, the Hmong and the Ioumein (Yao). Because of the Lao government's political policy, some highlanders have been relocated to live with other groups of Lao people.

The highlanders' ways of life center on farming in the high mountains. To reduce the amount of deforestation, some highlanders have been trained to do lowland rice planting (transplanting). Highlanders eat regular rice and vegetables. Most of them raise pigs for food. They like to eat greasy, soupy food. They do not like to eat uncooked food as the lowlanders do. Sometimes they mix water with their rice. They make a special kind of rice for social gatherings and festivals. The highlanders are good at embroidery, weaving cotton, and silver working, creating elaborate designs.

Thus we see that within the one country of Laos there are many different peoples.

Part 1: Lao Folktales

PART 2

Buddhist *Jātaka* and Moral Tales

Like people in other Buddhist countries, the Lao people's thoughts and conduct have been influenced by Buddha's teachings. This chapter emphasizes stories that are meant to teach people to behave properly according to those teachings, including *Jātaka* tales and moral tales.

Jātaka is a Pali word (*Xadouk* in Lao) referring to the "life stories of the Buddha." These stories were told by the Buddha to illustrate certain moral points in his sermons. Later, when his disciples recorded them in the collection called the *Dhamma,* or Buddhist teachings, the lives of some of Buddha's followers were included. The *Jātaka* tell of animals and humans in the many rebirths of the Buddha. Thus the main character in many *Jātaka* stories is assumed to be the Buddha in an earlier rebirth.

For a more detailed discussion of the *Jātaka,* see page 20.

PHRA WETSANDON XADOUK

Retold by Kongdeuane Nettavong, Vientiane, Laos. Translated by Wajuppa Tossa.

The following is the story of the rebirth of the Lord Buddha just previous to his incarnation as the Buddha. This story is recited in its entirety on the occasion of the Boun Phawet Festival each year. The recitation of the story in Boun Phawet starts early in the morning and ends at about eight in the evening. It must be completed within one day. First there is a sermon on the battle with Mara, the god of death and desire. This is followed by a recitation of a thousand verses of text in Pali. Pali is a script from India in which ancient, sacred texts are written. This can be read by learned monks. Pali verse is chanted by a monk (or monks). Then the audience throws puffed rice at the Buddha image installed in the public prayer hall. The monks then translate the sacred Pali text into comprehensible Lao. As the monks are reading the story, people donate money to the temple. The money is used for temple supplies and repairs.

This festival usually takes place in March, during the dry season. This is also the hottest time of the year. The symbolism of the water-giving powers of Vessantara's magic white elephant has a special potency at this time of year, when farmers wait anxiously for the life-giving rains and their return to planting rice in rain-soaked fields.

A long time ago in India there was a kingdom ruled by Thao Sanxai and Nang Phoutsadee. This king and queen had a son named Wetsandon. When it was the right occasion, he was married to Nang Matxee. Wetsandon and Nang Matxee had a son named Thao Xalee and a daughter named Nang Kanha. The kingdom was prosperous, with plenty of rain for planting because of an auspicious white elephant. This elephant caused good luck to come to whoever possessed it. One day Prince Wetsandon rode the white elephant to visit the people in the city. A group of Brahman from another country stopped the procession and begged the prince:

"Oh, please, your majesty, please help us. Our city is facing a serious drought problem. We have not had rain for many years and many months. Please give us your white elephant so that we could have rain."

The prince did not hesitate at all in saying yes to the group of people. He dismounted and readily gave them the magic elephant.

Upon hearing this news, the king and queen were in distress, but they loved the prince so much, they did not say anything. Not long after the elephant was given away, there were no rains in the city. The people could not begin their planting. They all blamed this problem on the prince. They marched to the city to ask the king to send the prince into exile for fear that he would give away more of the city's luck-bringing items. The king had to send the prince into exile to a jungle. The prince's wife, Matxee, insisted on bringing the royal children and accompanying the prince on this journey. So the entire family went into exile.

On the way to the jungle, many people came to beg for his possessions and belongings, and Prince Wetsandon gradually gave away everything. If anyone asked for something, the prince would not hesitate, but would give them what they needed. Finally, even the carriage was given away, and the family had to travel on foot. They eventually reached a mountain called Khao Wongkot. There they decided to stay. The prince vowed to live apart and meditate, so that he could accumulate enough merit to be reborn as the next Buddha. The prince stayed in one hut and his wife and children stayed in another one.

Everyday Nang Matxee would go out to gather some wild fruit to feed her family. One day Xuxouk, an old Brahman who was married to a young wife, appeared at the abode while Matxee was gone fruit gathering in the jungle. The Brahman asked Prince Wetsandon to give him his children. He wanted to take them home to be servants to his wife, as she complained of hard work at home. Again the prince had no hesitation in giving away what was his. He gave his own children to the Brahman. So the Brahman took the children and dragged them along out of the jungle.

When Matxee returned from her daily food gathering, she collapsed upon hearing the news. The god Indra rejoiced in this great merit making of the prince and decided to test the prince for the last time in his selfless giving. Indra descended from heaven, in disguise as an old Brahman, to ask for the prince's wife. Again the prince would not deny a request. He gave Matxee to the Brahman. As Prince Wetsandon was pouring lustrous water on Matxee and the Brahman as a sign of his consent, all celestial beings rejoiced, and Indra resumed his divine image in front of the prince. Indra then returned Matxee to the prince.

By this time, the Brahman Xuxouk and the royal children had accidentally arrived at King Sanxai's city. The children were recognized, and Xuxouk was given all kinds of treasures and food for bringing the royal children back. Xuxouk was elated and gobbled up so much of the food that he died of gluttony.

When the king learned the whereabouts of Prince Wetsandon, he sent a grand procession to bring the prince and Nang Matxee back to rule the kingdom. And thus the story ends happily.

THE TURTLE AND THE SWANS

Told by Phra Inta Kaweewong, Wat Sa-ahdsomboon, Roi-et Province, Thailand. Collected and re-told in English by Wajuppa Tossa.

This is a Jātaka to teach certain moral points to high-ranking people without embar-rassing them. The Buddha told this story to King Bhrahmadatta of Benares, who was so talkative that he would not let any of his advisors give him advice. Once he had heard this story, the king changed his behavior.

*O*nce a couple of swans, a husband and a wife, sighted a pond full of fish. So they flew down to have some fish, not knowing that a turtle was guarding the pond.

"Why are you eating fish in my pond without asking for my permission?" asked the turtle.

"Oh, does this pond belong to you?" replied the swans.

"Yes, I have been guarding this pond for a long time," said the turtle.

"We are so sorry. We thought nobody owned this pond," apologized the swans.

"Since this pond belongs to you, may we have some fish in your pond?" politely asked the swans.

"Now that you asked, you may have some fish in this pond," said the turtle.

After that, the swans visited the turtle every day. Soon they became fast friends. One day the swans thought they would do something nice for the turtle in return for sharing fish with them.

"Friend Turtle, we appreciate your sharing the fish with us. We would like to do some-thing nice for you in return. Is there anything we can do for you?"

The turtle had always had a dream that he could travel in the air and enjoy looking at the scenery from a different angle. So he asked, "Are you sure?"

"Yes," said the swans.

"My dream is that I might be able to fly high in the air and enjoy the scenery below," the turtle told his friends.

"Oh, that is not a problem for us. We can help you fly," said the swans.

"How? I don't have wings like you. I have this heavy shell on my back with these four short legs," said the turtle.

So the swans explained, "Well, we can get a long stick and hold on to the two ends with our beaks. You could bite hard on the middle. Then you can fly with us."

The turtle could hardly wait to fly with the swans.

"Yes, let's go, let's do that now," he said.

The swans held on tight to the two ends of the stick, and the turtle bit hard in the middle.

Before the swans took off, they said to their friend,

"Friend Turtle, be sure to keep biting on the stick. Don't ever open your mouth no matter what happens. Or you may fall onto the ground. And we won't be able to help you."

"Yes, I promise not to open my mouth," said the turtle.

So the swans flapped their wings and slowly lifted the turtle in the air.

The turtle looked down and saw the pond getting smaller and smaller.

He was very happy, but he kept his mouth shut.

He saw the top of the trees for the first time in his life.

He was very happy, but he kept his mouth shut.

"Oh, this is so much fun. I can't wait to tell my other turtle friends that I can fly!"

He was very happy, but he kept his mouth shut.

As they flew past a rice field, they saw a boy and a girl walking their buffaloes to graze on grass. The boy looked up and saw the turtle being carried aloft by two swans.

The boy pointed up. "Look, two swans are carrying a turtle."

The girl looked up and disagreed, "No, a turtle is carrying two swans."

"No, two swans are carrying a turtle," the boy insisted.

"Can't you see a turtle is carrying two swans?" cried the girl.

When the turtle heard what the argument was about, he thought,

"Yes, the girl is right. TURTLE IS CARRYING TWO SWANS."

He was very proud of himself, but he kept his mouth shut.

But then the boy's voice came loud and clear.

"No, two swans are carrying a turtle," said the boy, pointing up.

The turtle's pride was hurt, so he opened his mouth to argue with the boy.

Part 2: Buddhist *Jātaka* and Moral Tales

"TURTLE CARRYING SWAAAAA . . . ."

The turtle's body smashed onto the ground. His blood and guts went all over and splashed on the boy's armpit as he was pointing.

"Oh, this smells bad." The boy tried to wash and scrub his armpit, but no matter how hard he scrubbed and washed, the smell was still there.

The girl did not get splashed as badly as the boy.

Since then, boy's or men's armpits smell, and the smell is called *khi tao,* which means turtle poop!

But girl's and women's armpits do not smell as bad. At least that is what they say in Northeastern Thailand and Laos.

A FLYING LESSON

Told by Phra Sunantha Theerapanyo Phikkhu. Collected and retold in English by Wajuppa Tossa.

*O*nce the Buddha was born King of the Vultures. He was well revered and respected by all for his loving kindness, compassion, generosity, and devotion to his subjects and his own family. When he became a father, he was one of the best fathers. He brought up his son with love and warmth. When it was time for his son to learn to fly, he and his wife would teach the son to fly.

The first lesson was to fly from the nest to the ground. The king was proud to have such a strong and able son who could fly beautifully in his first lesson. Then the flying lesson would get higher and higher each day. They taught the son until he was strong enough to practice flying without the parents' supervision.

Each day, they would ask the son, "How high did you fly today, my son?"

"Oh, today I flew up to the top of the tallest tree in the forest, Father and Mother," came the answer from the son.

"Be careful to observe what you can see down below, my son," his mother would say.

"When the rice field seems as small as a human palm, the house as small as a buffalo dung pile, and the river as narrow as a human arm, you must not fly any higher," said his father.

"Yes, Father, Mother; I have not reached that height yet," said the son.

The next day, the son went out flying again. When he returned, his parents asked him again.

"How high did you fly today, my son?"

"Oh, Father, Mother, today I flew up high, but I have not reached that height that you mentioned yet," answered the son.

"Be careful to observe what you can see down below, my son," his mother would say.

"Remember when you see the rice field as small as a human palm, the house as small as a buffalo dung pile, and the river as narrow as a human arm, you must not fly any higher," said his father.

"Yes, Father, Mother; I haven't gone up that high yet," said the son again.

The next day, the son went out flying again.

He flew up higher and higher. He flew up very high, yet he was still not tired. He kept taking a higher and higher flight. Then he thought, "I should look down now to see if I can see the small rice field, the small house, and the narrow river."

The young vulture looked down. And lo and behold, the rice field was as small as a human palm, the house as small as a buffalo dung pile, and the river as narrow as a human arm.

"Yes! I did it. I can see the small rice field, the small house, and the narrow river. I have flown the highest flight any bird can." He was very happy and proud of what he could do.

"How wonderful it is that I could do it! Yet I am still not feeling tired at all. Perhaps my parents' warning was for some older birds," he thought.

"I could fly higher, for I am still young and strong," he told himself.

So, he flew up and up and up and up . . . .

All of a sudden, he felt his wings were fluttering, his body swaying here and there, his eyes growing dim. He then realized that in the higher atmosphere, strong winds came from every direction, and it was impossible to maintain his equilibrium.

That was the last thing he remembered. His body was hurled down fast, and faster, and faster. All he could remember was calling, "Father, Mother, help."

Back at his nest, the parents were waiting for their beloved son to return. They had no chance of asking how high he flew that day, or the next.

The young vulture woke up hanging on a branch of a tall tree far away from his own nest.

"Now I know what my parents meant by telling me not to fly too high. I should have stopped when the rice field looked as small as a human palm, the house as small as a buffalo dung pile, and the river as narrow as a human arm. They warned me. But I did not listen."

That was the lesson the young vulture learned. He promised himself that he would remember the lesson he had learned and teach it to his own children in the future: the "Flying Lesson."

THE THREE FRIENDS

Adapted from versions by Phra Inta Kaweewong, Wat Sa-ahdsomboon, Roi-et Province, Thailand, and Mantchanok Thongkanok, Muang Samsip School, Ubon Ratchathani, Thailand. Collected and retold in English by Wajuppa Tossa.

*O*nce upon a time, a long time ago, the elephant, the monkey, and the quail were friends. They lived in the banyan tree. In the morning the quail flew away, the monkey swung away, and the elephant walked away. In the evening the quail flew back, the monkey swung back, and the elephant walked back.

One day the elephant said, "We have been friends for a long time, but we have no leader among us."

The monkey said, "Let's find the leader."

The quail said, "Good idea! The oldest person can be our leader."

The elephant said, "Who is the oldest among us?"

The monkey said, "Who is the oldest among us?"

The quail said, "Who is the oldest among us? Let's go ask Banyan Tree."

The elephant said, "Banyan Tree, who is the oldest among us?"

The monkey said, "Banyan Tree, who is the oldest among us?"

The quail said, "Banyan Tree, who is the oldest among us?"

The banyan tree said, "Elephant, Monkey, and Quail, when did you first come here?"

The elephant said, "I came here when Banyan Tree was as tall as my stomach."

The monkey said, "I came here when Banyan Tree was as tall as my head."

The quail said, "I came here when Banyan Tree was a seed. I dropped the seed here. Then the seed sprouted and Banyan Tree grew, and grew, and grew to be a big tall tree."

The banyan tree said, "I know, the quail is the oldest. You are the leader."

The elephant and the monkey paid full respect to the quail as their leader. The quail was a good leader.

So the elephant, the monkey, and the quail lived happily ever after.

THE GOLDEN SWAN

Told by Phra Soubandit Duangwongsa, Wat Saphanthongnue, Vientiane, Laos. Collected and retold in English by Wajuppa Tossa.

Once, long ago, there was a family of three—father, mother, and daughter. Now it happened that the father died. But he was reborn as a swan with golden feathers. The swan recalled his previous life, when he had been born as a poor man. He could no longer lead his wife and daughter to have a happy life. He felt very sorry for his wife and daughter. So he flew to the house where his wife and daughter lived. He shook one of his golden feathers loose and let it fall into the house. When his daughter found the golden feather, she took it to sell in the market. The wife and the daughter survived on that money for a long while.

When the money was gone, the golden swan returned. He shook down another golden feather for the girl and her mother. One day the mother said to her daughter, "If the golden swan does not reappear soon, we will be starving again."

The daughter listened carefully when her mother continued, "This morning, if the golden swan comes again, you must catch him. Then we can pluck all his golden feathers. We shall be rich."

The daughter said, "Oh, mother, we should not do that. It will give the swan terrible pain."

"No, I don't care if the swan will be hurt or not. I am afraid of poverty," said the mother.

That day, the poor swan appeared, and the mother caught him. She started plucking out all the swan's feathers, against her daughter's wishes.

"Oh, I am going to be rich," she said. "Look at all these golden feathers. Daughter, come help me pull out the feathers."

"Oh, no, Mother. Please stop. Do you see how pained the swan looks?" cried the daughter. "And look, Mother, the feathers have turned into ordinary ones. They are not golden anymore."

It was true. The beautiful golden feathers turned ordinary as the mother yanked them out.

"What? What happened? Why don't you give me golden feathers, swan? Go away. Go away," cried the mother with tears of disappointment running down her cheeks.

Alas, the swan could no longer give them golden feathers. And the mother and daughter remained as poor as ever.

THE MAGIC WHITE SWAN

Told by Sivilay Sopha, Vientiane, Laos. Retold in English by Wajuppa Tossa.

A farmer went fishing one day. He had a long fishing net. Like other farmers, he wore a piece of cloth around his head. He cast his net, but he got nothing. He did it again and again, but he still got nothing. There was not a single fish. He cast his net once, twice, three times, but he got nothing. He cast his net for the last time and pulled up the net. He pulled and he pulled. "Oh, it is very heavy."

Then he found a white pebble in his net. It was the most beautiful pebble that he had ever seen. So he took the pebble home and placed it on the altar above his head. After dinner he went to sleep. The next day the white pebble had turned into a white swan. The swan approached the farmer and said, "I will take you to a place, a beautiful place, full of flowers. You can take whatever you like."

So the farmer climbed onto the swan's back and held tight. The swan began flapping its wings and flew off to the garden, with the farmer sitting on its back.

Once there the farmer enjoyed the garden. He picked one flower and felt that it was heavy. He picked the second one and it got heavier. He picked the third one and it was even heavier.

"Oh, I don't think I should pick any more flowers. It will be too heavy for the swan to fly and take me home."

So the swan took the farmer back home and disappeared. The flowers had turned into gold! The farmer became a rich man.

The news of his wealth reached the ears of his friend, who came to ask the farmer right away about how he had acquired his wealth. The farmer told his friend everything.

The next day his friend went to fish in the river with his long net.

He cast his net, but he got nothing. He cast his net once, twice, three times, but he still got nothing. He cast his net for the last time and pulled up the net. Then he found a white pebble in his net. He took the pebble home and placed it in his room.

The next day the pebble had turned into a beautiful white swan. The swan said to the second farmer, "I will take you somewhere today, to a flower garden."

So the man jumped on the swan's back, and the swan took off to the flower garden. Once there the man picked the flowers, one, two, three. They were heavy. But he did not care.

"These will turn to gold. I want to pick a *lot*," he thought.

So he picked two armloads of flowers and went to the swan.

"Take me home now. I will put these away and I will come back for more."

The greedy man jumped on the swan's back. But it was very heavy, the swan could barely fly. The swan swayed left and right with the weight. With great difficulty he was able to take the man to his house.

The man jumped off the swan's back and said, "Now, wait here. Don't go away. I will go back to the garden and pick more flowers."

Then he took the flowers into his house, but when he came back out again, the exhausted swan had flown away.

"What? Oh well. I have plenty of golden flowers already." But when the greedy man went back inside his house, he discovered just a pile of ordinary flowers . . . no gold at all.

And that's the story.

About the *Jātakas*

In Thailand and Laos, the *Jātaka* tales are divided into five categories: *Nibat Xadouk, Atthakatha Xadouk, Dika Xadouk, Panyaat Xadouk, and Xadouk Mala. Nibat Xadouk* refers to stories in the *Tripitaka* (the "Three Baskets of Dhamma," the Buddhist scriptures, books 27 and 28). *Nibat* means Pali verse in the *Tripitaka.* Each *Nibat* consists of sections, and each section contains *Jātaka* tales. There are a total of 547 tales in the *Nibat Xadouk.*

Atthakatha Xadouk is a collection of stories recorded a thousand years after the Buddha's attainment of nirvana. The stories were written in prose to explain certain Pali verses from the 547 tales in the *Nibat Xadouk.* Some of these stories were completely new, and some were explanations or elaborations of short and unclear stories from the *Nibat Xadouk.* There are 547 stories in this collection as well.

Dika Xadouk is a collection of explanatory notes in simple Pali, comparing and contrasting the stories from the first two types and explaining Pali grammatical notes.

Panyaat Xadouk is a collection of prose stories in fifty sets of palm leaf manuscripts composed in Khmer by monks from Chiang Mai in northern Thailand. These stories are not the *Jātaka* tales in the Buddhist scriptures, but rather mostly local folktales as well as folktales from Egypt and Persia. Some could be found in the *Panjatantra* stories as well. The monks who related the stories made them sound like the *Jātaka* tales for teaching purposes.

Xadouk Mala are the Mahayana Buddhist *Jātaka* tales translated from Sanskrit texts. Most of the stories contain details on the association of characters to the persons in the Buddha's lifetime. These stories were composed to be parts of sermons for teaching. Stories in this collection are about various classes of people (high, middle, and low), describing their ways of life, clothing, beliefs, and customs. Some of these stories are used to help solve daily problems in people's lives as well. There are altogether 34 stories, 27 of which are the same as those in the 547 stories in the Buddhist scripture. Seven are new stories with no sources.

The *Jātaka* tales were told, retold, and composed for one common purpose, to teach. Thus they could be classed as moral tales as well. In Lao tradition there is also a set of stories that, although obviously not included in the Buddhist *Jātaka* tales, are intended to teach right conduct in society. These are called didactic chronicles because they are treated as true stories. The *Jātaka* tales are still told and retold in Laos as part of the Buddhist ritual called *Boun Phawet,* the celebration of Prince Vessandon (Pra Wetsandon), the previous life of the historical Buddha.

PART 3

Tales of Xiang Miang and Other Tricksters

Like the people in most Asian countries, the Lao people have great respect and consideration for their elders, Buddhist monks, high-ranking people, and royalty. They would not speak back to, disobey, or revolt against them in any way. However, in the imaginary world of folktales, subordinates can outwit or defeat higher authorities if the authorities are not just, or if they do not behave properly. In Lao tradition, the representative of subordinates is a notorious trickster named Xiang Miang. Xiang Miang stories, like other trickster tales, provide checks for society to reexamine the roles of elders, Buddhist monks, high-ranking people, and royalty.

THE BIRTH OF XIANG MIANG

Told by Jinda Duangjai, Kamalasai, Kalasin, Thailand. Collected and retold in English by Wajuppa Tossa.

This story's trick depends on words with double meanings. See the note at the tale's end for the double-meaning words.

*O*nce there was a city whose king wished to have a son, the heir to his throne. One night his queen had a dream. She dreamed that a gem and a red nutmeg log fell from heaven. The gem fell right down into the palace, but the nutmeg log flew away. Later, the nutmeg log flew right back to be in the palace in order to be together with the gem. The court astrologer made a prediction that the king and queen would have a son who would not be very healthy. The only way to solve the problem was to find a boy who was born at about the same time to bring up together with the royal son.

Not long after that, the queen delivered a son who was not quite healthy, as in the prediction. The king ordered all of his people to go out searching for the child who was born on the same day and at the same time as the little prince. They found a poor woman with a baby whose husband had died. They took her baby back to the palace, giving silver and gold as rewards to the poor woman.

The king was delighted to have the baby at first. They called the child Kham (gold) after his natural mother's name, Kham Hang. At about that time, a wife of one of the courtiers delivered a baby that was stillborn. The king ordered her to raise the baby boy until he grew up. The boy showed his wit and intelligence from the age of three.

When the boy was seventeen, the king called his son and this adopted son to his side. He asked the prince to take care of the adopted son. The prince must promise that when he became king, he would not punish his brother no matter what happened. After getting the promise from the prince, the king died. The adopted son was ordained to be a novice monk during the royal funeral. It is customary for a son to shave his head and take the robes of a monk during the funeral proceedings, to make merit for the deceased person, which will help the dead person in the afterlife. After the funeral, the prince became king, while the adopted son remained a novice monk.

There were many episodes of the adopted son's life while he was a novice, and one was related to how he got his name, Xiang Miang.

Xiang-Miang Tricks the Merchants

One day while the novice Kham was bathing in the river, there came some merchants who were bringing betel leaf and areca nuts to present to the king. They asked the novice, "How deep is the water?"

The novice answered, "I would not know how deep it is, as I cannot see through to the bottom of the river."

The merchants asked, "Can we cross the river?"

"No, no one can cross this river," the novice firmly replied.

"Don't fool us," said the merchants. "We can easily cross this river. Do you want to bet?" challenged the merchants, knowing that it was against the Buddhist disciplines to bet or gamble.

"Of course, I will bet that you cannot cross this river," said the novice.

"What are you going to put up as a stake in this betting?" asked the merchants.

"Well, I have no silver or gold to bet with you, nothing but my novice robes I am wearing," said the novice.

"All right, we shall take your robes," said the merchants, hoping to see the funny sight of a naked novice.

"How about you, what will you give me if you lose?" asked the novice.

"Well, you can have all our betel leaf and areca nuts that we were going to present to the king," said the merchants, seeing no chance of the novice winning.

"All right, now let's see you cross the river," said the novice.

The merchants carried all their boxes of betel leaf and areca nuts over their heads and swam across the river. Once they got to the river bank, they said, "Now, Novice, give me your robes. We have crossed the river."

"Oh, no," said the novice. "You did not cross the river, but you swam in the river. When I bet with you I said *khwam*,* which means 'to step across'. I bet that you would not be able to cross the river with one stride. And none of you could do that. Give me all your betel leaf and areca nuts NOW!" commanded the novice.

"Sorry, we cannot give you this box of betel leaf and areca nuts because they are for the royal storehouse. If you want it, you must come and get it from the king himself," replied the merchants.

With that, all the merchants went directly to the king. Once there they were surprised to see the novice sitting at the side of the king. They learned that the novice was actually the king's adopted brother.

The novice explained all that had happened and demanded he get all the betel leaf and areca nuts. The king asked the merchants to explain and then understood what happened. So he said to the merchants, "Now it is not right that a Buddhist novice would gamble in any way. However, since it was done, why don't you just give to Kham, *sii saa haa baht* as a fine."**

When the merchants came with five *baht* to pay to the novice, they were surprised. The novice put down four large baskets and five Buddhist monk's bowls.

"Now, please fill these baskets and bowls with betel leaf and areca nuts," demanded the novice. "You heard what the king said, that you have to pay a fine of four baskets and five bowls full."

The merchants were speechless. They quickly went to the king and asked for help. Once the story was told, the king understood how clever the novice was. So he ordered the baskets and the bowls to be filled with betel leaf and areca nuts. The novice then shared all of it with his friends in the court.

Not long after that, the king ordered the novice to resign from the Buddhist order and return to live in the palace grounds, since he had violated one of the Buddhist disciplines. After Kham resigned from the temple, the king promoted him to be in charge of the royal storehouse of betel leaf and areca nuts. And his royal title became Xiang Miang. *Xiang* is a title given to a layperson who has been a novice. *Miang* is the betel leaf and areca nut for chewing.

That's the story of the birth of Xiang Miang and how he got his name.

Note: Though Xiang Miang is related to the king in this tale, usually he is not considered to be a relative of the king he is tricking in the stories we give here.

---

*The word *khwam* means to "go" across. But it can also mean to "step" across.

** This could be taken to mean four (*sii*) or five (*haa*) *baht* coins. But it could also be interpreted to mean four baskets and five metal bowls full. One word for basket is *saa,* and the metal bowl used by monks to collect food is called a *baht*.

XIANG MIANG OUTWITS THE KING

Retold by Wajuppa Tossa.

Xiang Miang was a notorious trickster who was so clever that the king had to have him work in court. But the king did not really like Xiang Miang. So he tried to find occasions to outwit Xiang Miang.

One day the king thought of a plan.

He called a meeting and made an announcement.

"Today, I have a game to play. If anyone can make me jump in the pond, I will give a reward to him."

Everyone in the meeting was silent, for the king was the most powerful man in the kingdom.

They did not dare to accept the king's challenge.

So the king turned to Xiang Miang.

"How about you Xiang Miang? You are very clever; don't you want to try?"

Xiang Miang spoke politely and humbly, "Oh, Your Majesty, I am your humble servant. I would not dare to make you jump in the pond at all."

The king was delighted. He laughed loudly, slapping his hand on his knee.

But then Xiang Miang's voice stopped him from laughing.

"Your Majesty, I would not dare to make you jump in the pond. But if you were already in the pond, I am sure I could make Your Majesty come out of it."

The king then said, "All right," and jumped in the pond.

"Now, make me get out of the pond, Xiang Miang."

Xiang Miang smiled and said, "Well I don't have to do that, Your Majesty, because I have just won the bet by making you jump *in* the pond."

The king was dumbfounded, but he kept silent, waiting for another chance to outwit this court trickster.

XIANG MIANG FINDS THE BEST FOOD FOR THE KING

Told by Jinda Duangjai, Kamalasai, Kalasin, Thailand. Collected and retold in English by Wajuppa Tossa.

One day the king had a bad appetite. He could not eat any food. He became weak and unhappy. He called for Xiang Miang.

"Xiang Miang, you are so good at everything. Can you help me? You could get some medicine that will make me have a good appetite." The king challenged Xiang Miang.

"I will try my best, Your Majesty. I will go to search for the medicine for Your Majesty. I shall return soon. Please don't eat anything until I come with the medicine," replied Xiang Miang.

Xiang Miang went out of the palace late that morning. The king was waiting for the medicine. But Xiang Miang didn't return at lunch time. The king was getting hungrier and hungrier. Finally, he could no longer wait. So he ate everything that was presented to him. After eating he felt much better, but he was still waiting for Xiang Miang.

Xiang Miang took his time. He walked out of the palace slowly. He just went along on the road. He was not in a hurry to return for the king's lunch time. He went about doing this and that until sundown. Then he began to head back to the palace.

"So, you are back. Where is your medicine?" the king asked. He then said, "I was so hungry that I could not wait for you. I ate a lot of food."

"Your Majesty, hunger is the best medicine for the loss of appetite. When you are not hungry, you will not be able to eat much," said Xiang Miang.

"You are right again, Xiang Miang," the king said. He gave him rewards, but he was still trying to find an occasion to outwit this trickster.

XIANG MIANG AND THE SNAIL

Told by Kunthari Saichua, grade one, Anuban Ubon Ratchathani School, Ubon Ratchathani, Thailand. Collected and retold in English by Wajuppa Tossa.

Once when Xiang Miang was walking by a swamp near his village, he saw a snail moving slowly along the edge of the pond.

"Aha, ha, ha, ha, Snail, you walk so slowly. Where are you going?" asked Xiang Miang.

"I am going to the other edge of the swamp," answered the snail.

"Ha, ha, ha . . . I figure it must take you one month to reach the other edge of the swamp," said Xiang Miang. With that Xiang Miang laughed at the snail.

The snail looked up, feeling quite insulted. "Well, if you think you walk so fast, do you want a race?"

The snail's proposal tickled Xiang Miang so much that he laughed even louder. "Of course. When do you want to have a race? Now?" Xiang Miang challenged the snail.

The snail became quite nervous, but maintained his composure. "Oh, no, not now. I want you to have time to get in shape for the race," said the snail.

"What?" exclaimed Xiang Miang, annoyed.

"Why don't we have a race tomorrow, at this time, here?" said the snail.

"Sure," said Xiang Miang.

The snail became a little worried about the race. So he went to his snail relatives for help. Other snails were more than happy to help because they would like to see the day that Xiang Miang was outwitted.

The next day came. The snail was waiting at the edge of the swamp for Xiang Miang. When Xiang Miang arrived, the snail said,

"Xiang Miang, since I am so small, it might be difficult for you to see where I am in the race. Why don't you call my name after you have run for awhile and I will answer your call? You can call, 'Snail!' And I can answer, '*Kuuk!*' "

"All right, let's rehearse," agreed Xiang Miang. "Snail!"

"*Kuuk!*" answered the snail.

Then the race began. The snail began to move slowly, and Xiang Miang ran off as fast as he could. Then he looked back and could not see the snail. So he called, "Snail!"

"*Kuuk!*" came the snail's answer from way ahead of Xiang Miang.

"How can that snail go so fast? He is ahead of me. I have to run faster. I am sure I can catch up with him easily," said Xiang Miang confidently to himself.

He ran and ran and ran as fast as he could. After awhile, he looked back and could not see the snail. So he called, "Snail!"

"*Kuuk!*" came the snail's answer from way ahead of Xiang Miang.

Xiang Miang began to feel a little concerned. "Oh, no! he is ahead of me again. I have to run faster. I think I can still catch up with him," said Xiang Miang with some confidence. So he ran and ran and ran as fast as he could. Then he called, "Snail!"

"*Kuuk!*" came the snail's answer from way ahead of Xiang Miang.

Xiang Miang became very exhausted and worried. "Oh, no! Not again! He is ahead. I have to run even faster now," said Xiang Miang.

So he ran and ran and ran until legs could no longer carry him. As he was about to lose consciousness, he called weakly, "Snail!" And he heard faintly, "*Kuuk!*" ahead of him. As he passed out, he still wondered how the slow-moving snail could defeat him in that race.

The clever snail had made a plan with the other snails in the pond. Snails had placed themselves at intervals all around the edge of the pond. They were waiting for Xiang Miang's call. And all snails look and sound just alike. So from the starting line to the finish line, there was always a snail ready to answer Xiang Miang's "Snail?" with a loud "*Kuuk!*"

This is the first time that the trickster Xiang Miang was outwitted. And it was only a tiny snail who did it!

XIANG MIANG SEES THE KING'S FACE

English translation by Wajuppa Tossa, from a secondary student's version in an English and story-telling camp in Kosumwitthayasan School, Kosumphisai, Mahasarakham, Thailand.

*T*here was a rule in old times that no one would be able to look at the king's face. If any one was so curious as to take a glimpse at the king's face, the punishment would be that person's head.

Xiang Miang was very curious to know what the king looked like and why the king had set up such a silly rule. He thought about it very hard and waited for a chance of seeing the king's face.

One day the king was out in his village to visit the people. He wanted to find out how his people were doing and if they had any troubles. The king was curious also to find out what people ate for their meals. People came with the dishes that they liked the most to show the king. Nothing was very interesting. The king looked at the dishes and disregarded them.

Then Xiang Miang came to have an audience with the king. He prepared Chinese watercress vines boiled in brine. He took the longest vines and coiled them up in a bowl. They looked interesting to the king.

"Boy, what is that in your bowl?" asked the king.

"Oh, it's the most nutritious dish, Your Majesty," said Xiang Miang with his face turned down to the ground. "It's called boiled Chinese watercress vines," continued Xiang Miang.

"How do you eat that?" asked the king. "Show me how you eat it; I want to see," ordered the king.

"Before I eat this, Your Majesty must promise not to punish me if I break any rule," requested Xiang Miang. "Otherwise, I will not be able to show Your Majesty how to eat it."

"Come on, now, show me. I promise that you won't be punished in any way," confirmed the king.

So Xiang Miang picked up the vine and lifted up his face to drop the end of the vine in his mouth. As he was doing so, he could not help but see the king's face. He quickly chewed the Chinese watercress vine and turned his head back to face the ground again.

"Now, I don't wonder why the king does not allow anyone to look at his face," thought Xiang Miang. "His face looks just like a horse's face."

XIANG MIANG TRICKS THE KING

Told by Jinda Duangjai, Kamalasai, Kalasin, Thailand. Retold in English by Wajuppa Tossa.

In this tale Xiang Miang is the adopted brother of the king.

When Xiang Miang was promoted to be in charge of the royal storehouse of betel leaves and areca nuts, he lived on the palace grounds. Every once in awhile, the king would ask to see him. One day the king thought of a plan to outwit Xiang Miang.

"Xiang Miang, I heard that you are the trickiest person in the city. Is it true?" asked the king.

"I am not sure, Your Majesty," replied Xiang Miang.

"Well, today I want to see if you could trick me," said the king.

"Oh, no, I dare not trick Your Majesty," said Xiang Miang.

The king laughed and said, "Well, I think you are tricky; come now, trick me."

Xiang Miang joined his hands together as if about to perform a trick. Then he stopped. "I am afraid that it's not proper for me to trick your majesty right in front of you. It would be better if Your Majesty turned around and didn't look at me while I do this."

"All right." The king then turned around and said, "Now Xiang Miang, trick me. My face is turned away."

"Oh, Your Majesty, but I have tricked you already," said Xiang Miang. "I made you turn around!"

The king laughed heartily at Xiang Miang's wit, waiting for a chance to outwit Xiang Miang.

THE NOVICE AND THE ABBOT

Told by Suched Somsa, a storytelling student at Mahasarakham University, Mahasarakham, Thailand. Collected and retold in English by Wajuppa Tossa.

Many tales are told about the novice who tricks his abbot. Often that novice is assumed to be Xiang Miang.

*J*n the old days, parents sent their sons to live in the temple so that they could learn to read and write and absorb the Buddhist precepts. Some of them were ordained as novices; others could just stay as temple boys without ordination. The young novices would serve the older monks or the abbot of a temple. Early in the morning, they would walk with the abbot or the monk through the village carrying alms, offerings from villagers. If they could not go, they would sweep or clean the temple grounds and the *kuti,* the living quarters of the monks or the abbot.

One day the abbot was going out to receive alms from the villagers and the novice was not ready, so the abbot said to him, "Well, if you are not coming with me, you must sweep the temple grounds very well. Make sure that you don't let any chickens come near my living quarter."

"Yes, I will do my best," said the novice.

"Now, run along and get the broom and begin sweeping. Remember, if there are any chicken droppings near my *kuti,* you will have to lick them clean," the abbot said firmly.

"Yes, sire," said the novice, feeling a little annoyed at the abbot's final comment.

Once the abbot was gone, the novice swept the temple grounds and the *kuti* clean. Then he thought of a trick to play on the nagging abbot. He boiled brown sugar until it was very thick and dropped it on various spots near the abbot's *kuti.* After a while the brown sugar hardened and looked exactly like chicken droppings. Then the novice sat and waited for the abbot.

Later that morning, when the abbot returned to his *kuti*, he saw the little drops all over the place, and he became very mad.

"Novice, come here. Look at all these droppings. Remember what I told you? Come and lick all of the droppings clean now," commanded the abbot.

The novice ran quickly to the abbot and pretended to be upset. "Oh, no, that bad multi-colored rooster did it again. I will lick these droppings clean now."

So he stooped down and began licking the first drop. "Oh, wow, this is sweet." Then, he continued licking with zest. While licking he kept saying "Oh, this is good. So sweet, so sweet."

The abbot looked at him, puzzled. When the novice was about to lick the last dropping, the abbot could no longer control his curiosity. He said, "Stop, wait, Novice. Is it really sweet?"

"Yes, sire. It's really sweet, like brown sugar, I must say," said the novice.

The abbot was quite old, and he always liked to eat sweet things after meals. That day, no one had offered dessert in his alms bowl. So he said, "Well, if it is so sweet, let me try that last drop."

"Sure," said the boy. So the abbot stooped down and licked that drop until it was all gone.

"Wow, it was really sweet. Now, Novice, tomorrow, get that multicolored rooster here and make him drop more deliciously sweet droppings here," commanded the abbot.

So the next day, the abbot went to take alms in the village as usual, but he could not wait to get back to his *kuti* to have more of the delicious chicken droppings for dessert. The novice happily followed the abbot's command.

When the abbot got back to his *kuti,* he said, "Now don't you touch those droppings. I will have them after my morning meal."

After his meal, the abbot began licking the first drop. "Gaggg, this smells and tastes bad. It's not like the drop I had yesterday. Novice, what's wrong?" he asked.

"Oh, that must not be the multicolored rooster's droppings. Another chicken must have come round to drop without my knowledge. Please try the next one," suggested the novice.

And so the abbot tried almost every dropping, before he realized that he had been fooled.

THE ABBOT AND THE NOVICE CARRY SALT

Told by a storytelling student at Mahasarakham University, Mahasarakham, Thailand. Collected and
retold in English by Wajuppa Tossa.

*Here is another story of a tricky novice. Many stories are told about this tricky novice.
Sometimes he is named as Xiang Miang, but often no name is given.*

*I*n rural villages, salt is hard to find sometimes. In these villages, people save salt
for very important occasions. One time a family from another far village invited
the abbot to give a sermon in their house-warming ceremony. The abbot borrowed a horse
from the people in his village and went on the long trip with his novice. After the sermon,
the owner of the house gave salt as a gift for the monk to take back.

The abbot was riding on a horse and the little novice was carrying the heavy baskets of
salt and walking behind the horse. The sun was shining brightly and it was very hot. The abbot began to complain.

"Oh, how far is it before we get back to our temple, Novice?" asked the abbot. "Oh, it's
so hot and uncomfortable."

The little novice realized that it was hot and uncomfortable, especially since he had to
carry two baskets of salt on his shoulder. But he pretended to carry the load of salt with ease
and to enjoy the scenery and not show that it was hot.

"Oh, it's nice and cool for me, sir. I get the shade from the horse. And the load is light,"
said the novice.

"Really?" asked the abbot, wishing to be more comfortable.

"Yes, really!" answered the novice. "I would not change my place for anything, sir,"
continued the novice.

"Well, now you must change places with me. I don't want to ride on this uncomfortable and bumpy horseback anymore," stated the abbot. "I want to walk and carry that load in
the shade. You get on the horse and ride it now."

"Oh, sir, please, please, let me go on like this. It's so nice. Please," said the novice, pretending to beg.

The abbot stopped his horse and said, "Now stop, Novice, and put that load down. I am going to dismount the horse."

The novice pretended to stop reluctantly, and the abbot dismounted the horse.

"Now get on the horseback. Give me that load!" commanded the abbot.

"All right, if you insist," said the novice.

He rode on the horse happily, but pretending to be uncomfortable, and he complained.

"Oh, it's so hot and bumpy; I wish I could walk again," complained the novice.

The abbot put the load on his shoulder and began walking. It was a heavy load, and it was even hotter than when he was just riding on the horse. But he could not complain, as it was he who had demanded the change of place. So they went on their journey until they got halfway to the temple. The abbot could bear it no longer, so he said, "Now, Novice, let's take a break under the shade of that tree near that little pond."

"All right, sire," said the novice, stopping the horse and dismounting. He then tied the horse to a tree. By the time he was finished, the abbot was about to fall asleep under another tree a little farther from the pond. The little novice came to him and said, "Sire, are we going to take a little nap?"

"Yes, we are; I am a bit tired. You can take a nap, if you like," said the abbot.

"Oh, no, we cannot take a nap without hiding our salt first," said the novice, seeing a chance of mischief.

"Go ahead, hide it in a safe place, then. How about behind the bush there?" asked the abbot.

"Oh, no, that's too conspicuous, sire; we should hide it in the pond. I am sure no thief would think of looking in the water," suggested the novice.

"Good idea; go right ahead. I am going to take a short nap now," said the abbot, falling sound asleep.

So the little novice put the two baskets of salt in the water and prepared a lot of leaves for mischief purposes. Then he took a nap.

He made sure that he would wake up before the abbot. Of course by this time the water had dissolved all of the salt in the baskets. When the novice woke up, he pulled up the empty baskets from the water and put a lot of leaves in them to look like the leaves were covering the salt. When he was finished, he woke up the abbot.

"Sire, it's getting late. Let's go home," he said.

The abbot woke up and said, "Now, I want to share the pleasure of carrying the salt baskets and walking with you. I will take the uncomfortable seat on the horse until we get to the temple," said the abbot.

"I would be more than happy to do so, sire," said the novice as he picked up the load and put it on his shoulder as the abbot mounted the horse.

The load was light, and the walk was surely easy for the novice. He skipped and walked alternately with delight. The abbot just wondered why.

It was late in the evening by the time they got back to the temple. Once they got to the temple, the abbot dismounted from the horse and went to sleep. The novice returned the horse to the owner, put the baskets in a corner of the living quarters, and went to sleep as well.

The next morning the abbot woke up, took his alms bowl, and went to take alms from the villagers. The novice followed behind him. People were waiting to offer food to the monk on the side of the road. The abbot began to address them.

"Now, yesterday I went to another village and they gave us two baskets of salt. You can go to the temple and take a share for your cooking," offered the abbot.

"Thank you, Your Reverend," said the villagers.

After they finished taking the alms, the abbot and the novice returned to the temple. After their morning meal, the abbot said to the novice, "Now, Novice, bring out the salt. We will let the villagers come and take a share."

"Yes, sire," said the novice, bringing out the baskets full of leaves. He took out the leaves and pretended to be very surprised.

"Oh, No, Your Reverend, there is not a single grain of salt in the baskets," said the novice.

"What? What happened? Where has all the salt gone?" asked the abbot in great surprise.

"Oh, I knew it. The catfish in the pond must have eaten up all our salt," said the novice, showing great anger. "We have to take revenge on those naughty catfish."

"Yes, we have to go back and give a severe penalty to those catfish for stealing our salt," said the abbot. "Now let's go."

So the abbot and the novice headed toward the pond, walking so fast it looked like they were running. Once they got to the pond, the abbot ordered the novice, "Now, you must help me drain this pond so that we can get the catfish."

They drained the pond until there was only mud in the bottom of that pond. They could see fish struggling in the mud. The abbot caught the biggest catfish in the pond and said, "This must be the leader of all the fish in this pond. I will teach him a lesson."

"Yes, it's him, that big catfish. He stole our salt," said the novice, pointing his finger at the fish.

"I am sure he is big and fat because he has a lot of salt in his stomach," said the abbot.

"Now, hit his head, sire, to teach him a lesson," suggested the novice.

So the abbot hit the sides of the fish's head with his two palms before he let the fish go and let the water run back to the pond again. The water was muddy with blood color, but the blood was not from the fish. The fish had stuck out its sharp fins just as the abbot was about to hit it.

"Well," said the novice, "I guess you taught that fish a lesson!"

PART 4

Tales of Fools

THE DAY DREAMER

From *The Great Gourd of Heaven* by Samrit Buasisavath. Retold in English by Wajuppa Tossa.

*O*nce long ago, a man lived alone in a village not far from a city. He was not yet married. He often spent his time daydreaming.

He owned a beautiful pot, very old, which he kept locked away in a big box near his bed. Every morning and every night he would open the box and take the pot out. He touched it with his hands, stroking it again and again, saying quietly to himself, "Oh, my beautiful pot! You are my heart and I love you. You are very valuable and without you I couldn't be happy." And he would lose himself in his dreams.

One morning he had just come from outside, so he was holding his walking stick in his hand as he went to the box and took the pot out as usual. He held it, looking at it. Finally he put it on a table, quietly saying to himself, "Oh, my beautiful pot! You are the most beautiful pot in the world. You are very valuable, and if I sold you I would have a lot of money."

Suddenly a new idea came to him. He cried out involuntarily, "Oh yes, now I know what to do! What a wonderful thought!"

"I will sell my beautiful pot and become a millionaire!" he thought proudly.

"I shall have enough money to divide into two parts. One part shall be for my living expenses. What shall I do with the other part?

"I know! I'll buy a cow, big and strong. I'll look after her very well and she'll have a calf for me every year.

"Let me think, if I have her for ten years, how many cows will I have then? And this is not counting their calves as well; their numbers will increase every year!

"But supposing I now had ten cows! That's too many for me. Who will help me to look after them?

"I'll have to get married. Yes, that's it! I can see my wife, beautiful, and helpful to me. I'm not any common man; I'm a rich man and we live a loving and happy life.

"My beloved wife has given me a child—a son of course, and very handsome too.

"I love my son very much, and he is very clever. I love my wife and child as much as I love myself.

"I look after them well, providing them with food and clothing. They love me in return and we are a happy family . . . .

"Now my son has grown to be five years old. Next year he'll go to school. I've prepared everything for him, his books, pens, and pencils, all in a beautiful school bag. He is a very good boy, intelligent and quick to learn. He is never naughty and always obeys me.

"The day my family has been waiting for has arrived: my son goes to school. We are very pleased when I take him to the school, with his new school bag. He enjoys his time at school.

"I take him to school every day. One day I am so busy that I have no time to take him to school. But the school is not far from my home, so I let him go to school alone. I feel restless while he is away at school.

"In the afternoon of that day I wait for him at the door of my house. There he is! He is coming now, alone. Suddenly there is a dog running after him. It bites him! I am angry with the dog and cry out, 'You good for nothing dog, how dare you bite my son!' I turn quickly to hit it with my walking stick, like this! . . . Like this!"

But there were no cows, no wife, no son, and finally, no dog at all where he stood. There was only the beautiful pot in front of him and the walking stick in his hands. Thinking about the dog, he hit the pot with all his might, and it broke into many pieces!

Suddenly he woke up, frightened, from the daydream. What could he do? His pot was broken. He wept with sadness, whispering to himself, "Oh dear, I have lost all hope. My beautiful pot is broken. What shall I do? Oh God, look upon me now, and please help me. I have ruined everything in my life!"

But who could help him, because we know God will only help someone who can help himself? His pot was broken because he spent his time daydreaming, "building castles in the air."

THE CRESCENT MOON COMB

Told by Phatcharaphorn Dongruangsi, grade 11, Thetoon Village, Thailand, who heard the story from her grandmother. Collected and retold in English by Wajuppa Tossa.

*O*nce a man from a very remote village told his wife that he was going to go to town. He had to buy tools for fishing. He asked his wife what she wanted.

"Perhaps you could buy some candies for our five-year-old," she said. "By the way, would you buy a crescent-moon comb for me?"

"Oh, what a difficult name. I won't be able to remember it. I am quite forgetful, you know."

"Yes, I know. Now if you happen to forget, just look at the moon. It looks like that."

That day the moon was crescent shaped. So the husband left. At that time, there was no public transportation. He had to walk many nights before he reached town.

Once there, he bought what he needed for fishing. By the time he finished, he had forgotten what his wife asked him to buy. So he went to a shop.

He looked at this and that, and nothing reminded him of what his wife told him to buy.

The shopkeeper came and asked what he needed. He told the shopkeeper that he had forgotten. The shopkeeper pulled out various things to help him remember.

"Is it this lipstick?"

"No."

"Is it this purse?"

"No."

"Is it this spoon?"

"Spoon? Oh, I remember she told me to look at the moon."

The shopkeeper looked at the full moon. By the time the villager reached the town, the crescent moon had become full and round. The shopkeeper's eyes sparkled. He picked up a round object.

"Here you are. I bet this is what she wanted."

The shopkeeper wrapped the round object in brown paper and handed it to the villager. The villager paid and returned home happily.

Once home, his wife, his boy, his mother, and his father were there waiting for him.

"Here, have a candy." He gave his son a candy. The son tore off the wrapping and put the candy in his mouth.

"Have you got what I asked for?" the wife asked timidly.

"Oh, yes." The man put down his bag and rushed to get a drink from the water jar. "It is in my shoulder bag. Get it yourself."

The wife reached inside the bag, her heart beating fast, but stopped and said to her husband, "I don't find any crescent comb."

The husband came to the bag and reached inside. He pulled out the round thing wrapped in brown paper and gave it to her.

"Here you are."

The wife ripped the wrapping paper apart. The round object that the shopkeeper had wrapped up was a mirror. But no one in this family had ever seen a mirror before.

It was round like the moon but . . . . The wife looked into the mirror with dismay.

"What, old man, you are bad. You brought home a minor wife. This is bad." She screamed.

"What?" said his mother. "Let me see."

His wife handed the mirror to her mother-in-law.

"What? You are bad. You really brought home a minor wife. She is so old and wrinkled. How can you do that?"

The young boy, sitting near his grandmother, grabbed the mirror from his mother's hand and began throwing a fit.

"Grandpa, look, he is taking my candy."

The grandfather grabbed the mirror from his grandson.

"Let me see who this wicked person is."

"What? This is an old man. How can he try to take my grandson's candy?"

"He is making faces at me. This is bad. I will hit him with the handle of my knife here." The old man set the mirror on the ground and grabbed his knife.

"What! He is grabbing a knife to hit me, too."

With that the old man became so angry that he brought down the knife on the mirror until it was all broken.

"Now you cannot bother anybody any more."

And that's the story of the family who had never seen a crescent comb or a mirror in their lives . . . and still have neither.

Part 4: Tales of Fools

THE FOOLISH FAMILY

As told by ninth grader Khambao Thaenna, Mahasarakham, Thailand. Collected and retold in English by Wajuppa Tossa.

*O*nce there was a family of three: father, mother, and daughter. Every day the father and the mother would go to the field to work, while the daughter stayed home to cook the late morning meal for the family. After cooking, she would go to the field to deliver the meal and eat with her parents. This happened every single day.

One day the girl got up late because the night before she had gone to see a folk opera, a *lam mu*.* The girl got up, cooked the breakfast, and started carrying the food to the field for her parents. But the field was quite far away from home. As it was later than usual, the weather was quite warm, and because of lack of sleep, the girl became more and more tired. Finally she decided to stop and take a rest under the shade of a tree.

As she was sitting there, a cool breeze blew gently. The girl fell asleep. She began to dream of the lead actor in the folk opera. She dreamed that she was married to the actor and they lived together happily. Then she dreamed that she had a baby boy. In her dream everyone in her family was very happy about this. Then, while she was cooking, the boy ran around playing. When it was time for breakfast, she called her son. But he was nowhere to be seen. She hurried from the house and walked around the yard, but still she could not find the boy. When her husband came home and heard about how the son had disappeared, he began searching for him everywhere. Then he went to a pond near the field. He found the son, but he was dead. He had fallen in the pond while playing and was drowned. In the dream that had turned into a nightmare, she began to moan and cry for her lost son. The girl cried so much that she woke up crying.

Meanwhile, her parents began to feel hungry, but the daughter was not there yet. So the father said, "Why don't you go and see if our daughter has come out of the house? Perhaps she is sick." The wife walked away from the rice field. As she was heading home, she saw someone under a tree far away. She ran there and found that "the someone" was her own daughter, sitting and crying.

"What's wrong? Why are you crying?" the mother asked, feeling quite concerned.

"Oh, mother, *hue, hue, hue . . .*," the girl cried even louder upon her mother's enquiry.

"Come on, pull yourself together and answer my question," said the mother.

"Oh, mother, my son is dead. I dreamed that I was married to the folk opera actor and we had a son. While I was cooking, he ran to the pond and *hue, hue, hue,* he was drowned. I am so sorry because my son could have grown up to be a handsome folk opera actor, like his father." After explaining, the girl continued crying even louder.

Hearing the story, the mother began crying with a broken heart. "Oh, my dear grand-son, *hue, hue, hue* . . . . He would have grown up a young man and could have been ordained as a Buddhist monk. His merit as a monk would have delivered my soul from hell." The mother cried and wailed.

Back in the rice field, the father was waiting hungrily, looking at the path leading home. But no one from his family appeared. "What has happened to my wife and daughter? I can't wait any longer. I have to go see what has happened to them."

With that, the man walked hurriedly toward home. He saw ahead of him two women under the shade of a tree. He ran toward them and found that they were his wife and daugh-ter, sitting and crying as if someone had died.

"What happened to you two? Who hurt you to make you cry like this? Tell me and I will take care of him for you," said the husband.

The daughter was crying so hard that she could not answer his question. So the wife began to explain, sobbing.

"Oh, husband, my grandson is dead. Our daughter dreamed that she was married to a folk opera actor and they had a son. While she was cooking, the boy ran to the pond and *hue, hue, hue,* he was drowned. I am so sorry. He could have grown to be twenty and he could have been ordained as a Buddhist monk. His merit as a monk would have delivered our souls from hell. . . . *Hue, hue, hue* . . . ." The wife continued wailing and crying.

Upon hearing the story, the father began crying with a broken heart. "Oh, my dear grandson, *hue, hue, hue* . . . . He would have grown up a young man and he could have helped with hard work at home. I would have had a man to man relationship with him. What a pity, what a pity. . . ."

What a pity! Indeed. The three of them hugged each other and continued crying and moaning under the shade of that tree. For all we know, they might still be crying there now.

---

*The person who sings the *lam mu* (folk opera) is called *mo lam; mo* means a specialist. In the old times, only one singer could sing the entire story. But nowadays a group of singers perform, each taking a different role in the story. The play is accompanied by drum, gongs, *khaen,* cymbals, and xylophone.

PART 5

Animal Tales

WHY OWL HAS A FLAT HEAD AND YELLOW EYES

Told by Sivilay Sopha, Vientiane, Laos. Retold in English by Wajuppa Tossa.

*T*here were once two brothers, Hong Huat and Hong Hooy, who were going out to pick mushrooms in the forest. As they were picking mushrooms, a round fruit, called *maak khing* fell on their heads. This falling fruit made the two brothers angry, so they asked it, "*Maak Khing,* why did you fall on our heads?"

The *maak khing* answered, "Oh, it is not my fault. Squirrel bit my vine, so my fruit fell on your heads."

The two brothers went to ask Squirrel, "Squirrel, why did you bite *Maak Khing*'s vine? That made *Maak Khing* fall on our heads."

Squirrel answered, "Oh, it is not my fault. Snake coiled his body around my neck. I couldn't breathe, so I bit whatever was near."

The two brothers went to ask Snake, "Snake, why did you coil your body around Squirrel's neck? You suffocated Squirrel, so he bit the vine of *Maak Khing*. That made *Maak Khing* fall on our heads."

Snake answered, "Oh, it is not my fault. Ant bit my naval and made it swell up. I was hurt, so I squeezed whatever was near."

The two brothers went to ask the ant, "Ant, why did you bite Snake's navel? That hurt Snake. So Snake suffocated Squirrel. Squirrel bit the vine of *Maak Khing*. That made *Maak Khing* fall on our heads."

The ant answered, "Oh, it is not my fault. Pheasant scratched my nest, so I bit whatever was near."

The two brothers went to ask Pheasant, "Pheasant, why did you scratch Ant's nest? Ant bit Snake's navel. Snake suffocated Squirrel. Squirrel bit the vine of *Maak Khing*. That made *Maak Khing* fall on our heads."

Pheasant answered, "Oh, it is not my fault. Sesame Seeds flew up and blinded me. So I scratched Ant's nest. Ant bit Snake's navel. Snake suffocated Squirrel. Squirrel bit the vine of *Maak Khing*. That made *Maak Khing* fall on your heads."

The two brothers went to ask Sesame Seeds, "Sesame Seeds, why did you blind Pheasant's vision? That made Pheasant scratch Ant's nest. Ant bit Snake's navel. Snake suffocated Squirrel. Squirrel bit the vine of *Maak Khing*. That made *Maak Khing* fall on our heads."

Sesame Seeds answered, "Oh, it is not my fault. Squash fell on our vine. That made us fly up and blind Pheasant."

The two brothers went to ask Squash, "Squash, why did you fall on Sesame Seeds? That made Sesame Seeds blind Pheasant. Pheasant scratched Ant's nest. Ant bit Snake's navel. Snake suffocated Squirrel. Squirrel bit the vine of *Maak Khing*. That made *Maak Khing* fall on our heads."

Squash answered, "Oh, it is not my fault. Deer kicked my vine and that's why I fell on Sesame Seeds. Sesame Seeds blinded Pheasant. Pheasant scratched Ant's nest. Ant bit Snake's navel. Snake suffocated Squirrel. Squirrel bit the vine of *Maak Khing*. That made *Maak Khing* fall on your heads."

The two brothers went to ask Deer, "Deer, why did you kick Squash? Squash fell on Sesame Seeds. Sesame Seeds blinded Pheasant. Pheasant scratched Ant's nest. Ant bit Snake's navel. Snake suffocated Squirrel. Squirrel bit the vine of *Maak Khing*. That made *Maak Khing* fall on our heads."

Deer answered, "Oh, it is not my fault. I was sick and wanted to eat sour olives. So, I cried repeatedly, '*Yaak kin som kok de!* I want to eat the sour olive!' Owl heard my cry and told me, "When I see the sour olive, I will call you." One day Owl saw the sour olive tree, so he called, '*Keb kok, keb kok!* Come quick and pick sour olive! Come quick and pick sour olive!'

"So I followed the sounds of Owl, but then I heard his sound, '*Hok suk hok sak hok pak hok thaeng!* Push the lance, throw the lance, strike him with the lance, stab him with the lance.' I became frightened, so I kicked Squash's vine."

Everyone went to ask Owl, who answered, "Oh, it is not my fault."

But that was all Owl could say. He had no excuse. So finally, he admitted that he did frighten Deer.

So Owl was found guilty of causing a disturbance and was punished. His head was squeezed. He must paint around his eyes with turmeric. So to this day, the owl has a flat head and yellow eyes. He has no friend. He must find food only at night.

MAENG NGUAN, THE SINGING CRICKET

Told by Bounyok Saensunthone, Vientiane, Laos. Collected and retold in English by Wajuppa Tossa.

*O*ne night Indra heard a beautiful sound of music that went "*yong, yong, yong*." He was so pleased that he wanted to give a reward to the singer. So he said to his courtiers, "You must bring whoever sang that beautiful song last night to me. I wish to hear more of the beautiful song."

So the courtiers went out, making an announcement. "Whoever sang the beautiful song last night must come forward. The Great Indra wishes to hear more of your song."

Gecko stepped forward and said, "It's me that sang the beautiful song last night."

"Then tell me what I need to prepare for your performance tonight for the Great Indra," said one of the courtiers.

"Oh, you must prepare a good size bamboo pipe and hang it on a pillar at the Great Indra's hall," said Gecko.

All was done before night fell. When night fell, Gecko crawled up to heaven, then went inside the bamboo pipe and began his song, "*thod, thod, thod, kapkae, kapkae, kapkae . . . .*"

The Great Indra then said, "Oh, you sang a beautiful song. I will give you a multicolored vest to wear."

Since then Gecko has had a multicolored body. Then Gecko went down to earth.

In the evening, the Great Indra again heard, "*yong, yong, yong*." The beautiful song again! "Gecko's song last night was beautiful, but this one is more heavenly." So he said to his courtiers, "Do you know that I still hear the beautiful song? The one I heard before Gecko came to sing? Please go to find the singer for me."

So the courtiers went out, making the same announcement. "Whoever sang a beautiful song last night must come forward. The Great Indra wishes to hear more of your song."

Bullfrog stepped forward and said, "It's me that sang the beautiful song last night."

"Then tell me what I need to prepare for your performance tonight for the Great Indra," said one of the courtiers.

"Oh, you must prepare a large bowl of water and place it at the foot of the stairs of the Great Indra's hall," said Bullfrog.

All was done before night fell. When night fell, Bullfrog crawled up to heaven and then into the bowl of water and began his song, "*hueng aaang, hueng aaang, hueng aaang.*"

The Great Indra then said, "Oh, you sang a beautiful song. I will give you a striped vest to wear."

Since then Bullfrog has had a striped body. Then Bullfrog went down to earth.

In the evening, the Great Indra again heard, "*yong, yong, yong.*" The beautiful song again! "Bullfrog's song last night was beautiful. But this one is heavenly." So he said to his courtiers, "Do you know that I still hear the beautiful song? The one I heard before Bullfrog came to sing? Please go to find the singer for me."

This time the courtiers came across Maeng Nguan, the singing cricket. So they asked, "Did you sing a beautiful song last night?"

"Yes, I did. Why do you ask?" said Maeng Nguan, the singing cricket.

"Oh, the Great Indra wants to hear you sing again tonight. Would you come?"

"Yes, I will come," said Maeng Nguan, the singing cricket.

"Then tell me what I need to prepare for your performance tonight for the Great Indra," asked one of the courtiers.

"Oh, absolutely nothing. I will just fly to light on a pillar of the Great Indra's hall and sing," said Maeng Nguan, the singing cricket.

So that night Maeng Nguan, the singing cricket, flew up to heaven and then to light on a pillar of the Great Indra's hall and began singing, "*yong, yong, yong.*"

When Indra heard that song, he felt so delighted that he came out of his hall.

"Who sang that heavenly song?" he asked.

"Oh, it is me, Maeng Nguan, the singing cricket, my lord," Maeng Nguan said humbly.

"Then I will give you gifts," said Indra. "From now on you will be able to see both day and night. And you don't have to eat any ordinary food. You may enjoy heavenly food . . . dewdrops from heaven," said Indra.

"Thank you, my lord," said Maeng Nguan.

Since then Maeng Nguan, the singing cricket, can see both day and night and enjoys heavenly food . . . dewdrops from heaven.

And he continues singing his song: "*yong, yong, yong, yong, yong, yong, yong, yong.*"

WHY DOG LIFTS HIS LEG

Told by Bounyok Saensounthone, Vientiane, Laos. Collected and retold in English by Wajuppa Tossa.

*O*nce Dog had three legs. He was not happy with that because he could not run as fast as other animals and could not jump as far or as high as others who had four legs. So he went up to the Great Indra's heaven to ask for his fourth leg.

"Oh, Great Indra, please give me the fourth leg like you did for other animals," pleaded Dog.

The Great Indra said, "Well, there are no legs left. I have given them all away to the other animals that came earlier. You are too late, Dog."

"Oh, please, Great Indra, please give it to me. If I don't get my fourth leg, I won't go down to earth," insisted Dog.

"I don't have any more legs to give you. I have given all the legs away. All I have now are the legs of my stool."

But Dog kept pleading. "I just *have* to have a fourth leg. *Please,* Indra!"

Finally Indra relented. "Well, since you insist, you can take one of the legs of my stool."

"Oh, thanks so much, Great Indra. Now I can jump as high or as far as others and I can run as fast as them too," said Dog.

"Now that you have the leg of my stool, Dog, you must promise to keep it as clean as possible. Don't you ever soil it in any way," commanded Indra.

"Yes, Sire," confirmed Dog. "I will always take excellent care of this leg. And if I have to pee, I will lift my fourth leg up to keep it clean."

And to this day, that is just what Dog does. Watch. You will see what good care Dog takes of that special leg.

THE TIGER'S STRIPES

Told by Phra Sunantha Theeraphanyo, Vientiane, Laos. Collected and retold in English by Wajuppa Tossa.

*O*nce, long ago, there was a farmer. His rice fields were far from the village and near the deep forest. Each day he would go out to work in the field with the help of his huge buffalo.

Later a tiger came to live in the forest near the farmer's rice fields. He considered himself king of the forest.

One day the tiger saw the buffalo dragging a plough, with the farmer behind. The tiger thought to himself, "What a funny sight, the huge buffalo being a slave of the human, who is so small."

He watched, and he laughed at the sight day after day. Finally, he could not help himself. He approached the buffalo, which was tied to a tree while the farmer rested in the shade of his shelter.

"Hey, Buffalo! Why are you so foolish, working for the human who is so small? You are much larger in size."

The buffalo replied, "How can I be otherwise, when the human has *panya* [cleverness and wisdom]?"

When the tiger heard the word *panya*, he laughed and said, "*Panya?* Ha, ha, ha! I want to try the human *panya.*"

When the farmer came to bring the buffalo to work, the tiger approached the farmer and said, "Oh, Farmer, I heard the buffalo talk about your *panya*. I want to try your *panya*. We will see who is better, between you and I. I also want to see what *panya* looks like."

"If you want to see my *panya*, you must change place with my buffalo. Then you will see what my *panya* looks like," said the farmer.

The tiger was so curious to know what *panya* was that he agreed to change places with the buffalo. After being tied to the plough, he dragged it along the fields, with the farmer directing behind. It did not take long for the tiger to feel exhausted. So he said to the farmer. "Farmer, I am tired now. Tell me where your *panya* is and show it to me."

"Oh, I am sorry. I didn't bring it with me. I left it in the shelter," replied the farmer.

Hearing that, the tiger began to make plans. He would ask the farmer to go and get his *panya*. While the farmer was gone, he would eat the buffalo. He was getting a little hungry.

The farmer asked the tiger, "Do you really want to see my *panya*?"

"Yes, I really want to see it. Please go and get it for me quickly," replied the tiger.

"All right. I will go and get it for you, but I have one condition. I need to tie you to the big tree here before I go. My *panya* is truly afraid of the tiger. If I don't tie you up, it might run away before I could show it to you. If my *panya* sees that you are tied, it would not run away. Then you will see my *panya* face to face and you can see it all you want."

The tiger was so eager to see *panya* that he agreed to let the farmer tie him to the big tree. After doing so, the farmer left. He came back with ten bundles of rice straw. The tiger asked the farmer, "Where is your *panya*?"

The farmer replied, "This is my *panya*. I tricked you into letting me tie you up to this tree by using my *panya*. I know that you planned to eat my buffalo when I was gone. So I tied you up so that you would not be able to eat my buffalo."

The tiger now realized that he had been tricked and that the human is truly clever. There was no way he could outwit the human, because man possesses *panya*.

The farmer covered the tiger with rice straw and set it on fire. The tiger struggled until he was free, but the rope had burned into his skin and left stripes across his body. Because of that tigers have stripes to this very day.

WHY PYTHONS ARE NOT POISONOUS

Told by Bounyok Saensounthone, Vientiane, Laos. Collected and retold in English by Wajuppa Tossa.

*O*nce, long ago, pythons were the most venomous snakes. It was believed that the pythons could kill others even by biting on their footprints.

One day Python went to find food in a pond. He trapped many fish. It was a very fertile pond, so he kept eating and eating, but before the fish were finished he was full. So he left some fish for later and went away.

In the village there was a man by the name of Bo; people called him Ta Bo.* One day Ta Bo came to the pond and found Python's trapped fish.

"Wow, I am a lucky man today," he thought. So he took all the fish home.

The next day Python came to the pond, hoping to finish up his trapped fish. He found no fish left. He was so humiliated that he vowed to take revenge on the one who took his fish.

"I'll have to see footprints around here," he thought. Then he found a lot of human footprints.

"Aha, these must be the thief's footprints," he said. With that, he bit hard on one of the footprints.

Back home, Ta Bo fell down dead instantly.

When people heard that he had died, they came to help set up the funeral wake. Some people who did not know about it began to wonder where everyone was heading to.

"Where are you going?" they asked.

"Oh, Ta Bo *tai*, we are going to his house," came the answer. They meant "Ta Bo is dead (*tai*)."

Now Python overheard this. To Python it sounded like they said, "Ta (grandfather) bo (NOT) *tai* (dead)."

Python was very upset. "Why didn't that grandfather die? I bit his footprint. I must not be poisonous any more. My venom couldn't even kill an old grandpa! What use is this weak venom?"

And unhappy Python just spit all of his useless venom out into the pond and went away.

But Cobra, Scorpion, Centipede, and other animals saw what had happened. They all rushed up to the pond and began to take in Python's discarded poison.

Because of this, there are many poisonous creatures in Laos today. But the python is not one of them!

Bo is pronounced like <u>law;</u> it means "not." *Ta* means grandpa.

THE BALDHEADED LESSER ADJUTANT STORK, NOK KAXOUM HOU LAAN

Told by Bounyok Saensounthone, Vientiane, Laos. Collected and retold in English by Wajuppa Tossa.

*O*nce Nok Kaxoum went to eat fish in a pond. That day he happened to be in a pond with very many fish. He enjoyed eating the fish so much that he forgot to watch where the sun was. By the time he finished eating, it was completely dark. He could not find his way home to his nest.

At the same time Stork was also lost in the forest. So he went to the mynah bird to ask for refuge.

"Can I sleep in your nest until dawn comes?' he asked Mynah.

"Oh, no, you cannot. You are so big; you might sit on my little birdies," said Mynah.

"Oh, I won't sleep in your *nest*. I will just sleep on the porch. I will also be careful," said Stork, and then he went to sleep.

All this time Nok Kaxoum was still wandering in the forest. Nok Xaikwuak (the wood-pecker) heard the noise and became so frightened that he pulled out his sword, making the noise "*kwua ua uak.*"

Upon hearing Nok Xaikwuak's sound of pulling out the sword from his sheath, Talum bird beat his gong, "*mong meng, mong meng.*"

The sound was so loud that it frightened Stork. He woke up with a start, ran into Mynah's bird's nest, and stepped on Mynah bird's baby.

Mynah bird was so upset that she went to ask Swan, king of the birds, to judge the case.

"Your Majesty, I let Stork sleep on my porch, but he just ran inside the nest and stepped on my baby," reported Mynah.

"Why did you step on Mynah's baby, Stork?" inquired Swan.

"Oh, Your Majesty, it's not my fault. I heard the sound of a gong being beaten by Talum bird and was so frightened that I ran and accidentally stepped on Mynah's baby," explained Stork.

"All right, now bring Talum bird here," ordered Swan.

Once Talum bird was there, Swan asked, "Talum bird, why did you sound your gong so late at night? The sound truly frightened Stork, and he ran into Mynah's nest and stepped on her baby."

"Oh, Your Majesty, it's not my fault. I heard the sound of Xaikwuak pulling his sword from the sheath and was so frightened that I beat my gong so loudly that it frightened Stork, who ran and stepped on the Mynah's baby," explained Talum bird.

"All right, now bring Xaikwuak bird here," ordered Swan.

Once Xaikwuak bird was there, Swan asked, "Xaikwuak, why did you pull out your sword that made a frightening sound in the middle of night? The sound truly frightened Talum bird, and he beat his gong so loudly that it frightened Stork, who ran and stepped on Mynah's baby."

"Oh, Your Majesty, it's not my fault. I heard the sound of Kaxoum bird wandering in the forest in the middle of the night, and I thought it was a thief or robber. I was so frightened that I pulled out my sword from the sheath. The sound frightened Talum bird so much that he beat his gong and frightened Stork, who ran and stepped on Mynah's baby," explained Xaikwuak bird.

"All right, now bring Kaxoum bird here," ordered Swan.

Once Kaxoum bird was there, Swan asked, "Kaxoum, why did you wander in the forest in the middle of the night? Your sound frightened Xaikwuak bird so much that he pulled out his sword and made a frightening sound in the middle of night. The sound truly frightened Talum bird, who beat his gong so loudly that it frightened Stork, who ran and stepped on Mynah's baby."

"Oh, Your Majesty, I couldn't find my way home as it was dark. Ah . . . I overly enjoyed eating the fish after the rain until it was dark," said Kaxoum bird.

"Aha, so it is you who is the root cause of Mynah's trouble," said Swan.

"Oh, I admit it, Your Majesty," agreed Kaxoum bird.

"Now, Mynah, you may fine Kaxoum bird," commanded Swan.

"Oh, I don't have anything to give to Mynah, Your Majesty," pleaded Kaxoum.

"Then, Mynah, you may push Kaxoum's head down and pull out all the feathers on his head. That can be his fine," commanded Swan.

So Mynah did. She pulled out almost every single feather until there were only three pieces left. Then she heard poor Kaxoum bird pleading, "Please, my dear Mynah, please leave me some feathers so that I can still court lady Kaxoum birds."

"All right, since you asked, I will leave you three pieces on your head," said Mynah.

Kaxoum bird was so embarrassed by his bald head that he ran away. He went to stay with a *rishi* hermit, who was meditating for three months during the Buddhist Lent. He took care of the *rishi* for three months so well that the *rishi* asked what he would like as his reward.

"Now Kaxoum, tell me, what would you like in return for your work for me during the Buddhist Lent?" asked the *rishi*.

Kaxoum was more than elated to tell the *rishi* that he would like his feathers back on his head.

"All right, you must alight on the edge of the well before dawn. Once you see the first ray of dawn, you must jump in the well, reciting, '*Ohm seb*'," said the *rishi*. "Remember, don't say the word, '*Maha seb*,' which will take away your feathers," the *rishi* instructed the bird.

"Oh, thank you very much, Your Holiness," said Kaxoum bird with gratitude.

He went early in the morning before sunrise to alight at the edge of the well. Once the first ray of the sun appeared, he jumped in the well, chanting, "*Ohm seb*."

When he came out of the water, he had more than enough feathers on his head. But it seemed to him that he had *too many* feathers now.

"Hmm, I should take a few out. I will jump in the well again, saying softly, "*Maha seb*."

Once he emerged from the water, all his feathers were gone, except for the three pieces. "Oh, no! Too many came out!"

He jumped in the well again, saying, "*Ohm seb*," but this time nothing happened.

Kaxoum bird jumped in the well over and over again, making the incantation until it was noon. Still he had not got his feathers back. So he went to the *rishi* to make a report.

"What happened? Why do you have the same feathers?" asked the *rishi*.

"Oh, Your Holiness, I did as you instructed and got *too many* feathers. So I jumped in again chanting with a tiny voice, '*Maha seb*,' hoping to take a few feathers out, but I ended up this way, no matter how many times I jumped in again saying, '*Ohm seb*'," explained Kaxoum bird.

"I see. It happened this way because you disobeyed my instructions," concluded the *rishi*.

So to this day, Kaxoum bird has a bald head, with just three feathers sticking out.

And this is the origin of the Lao saying, "*huo laan luen khuu*" or "Your head is balder than your teacher's!" In other words, if you don't obey the instructions of your teachers, you will lose out because of it. Kaxoum bird became bald because he did not follow the instructions of his teacher.

PART 6

Riddle Tales

NINE BAMBOO CLUMPS

Told by Phra Wiangsamai, Vientiane, Laos. Collected and retold in English by Wajuppa Tossa.

*O*nce there was a family of four: father, mother, and two sons. When the sons were young boys, the parents died. The two sons became orphans. They had to make a living by begging or finding forest food to trade or sell for necessary things in their lives.

One day they went into the forest to look for forest items for sale. It was a strange day for the boys, for they could not find anything worth selling or trading. So they kept walking deeper and deeper into the dark forest. Yet they still could not find anything. Finally, they decided to go home empty handed. However, as they were turning around to go back, the way looked different. They kept walking this way and that way, but none of the ways led them out of the dark and deep forest of bamboo trees.

The younger brother began to cry, "Oh, Big Brother, I think we will die in this forest."

The older brother tried to console his little brother, "Don't worry; we will find a way out." As he was saying so, he could find no way out at all. He felt hopeless. So he said to his little brother,

"Now, Little Brother, I think the god, Phya In, will help us. We must sit down and pray to him."

So the two brothers sat down, put their palms together in prayer gestures, and closed their eyes before making their wish.

"Oh, please, Phya In, please help us to get out of this dark and deep forest. We promise to be good and kind to all creatures on earth."

Phya In, in heaven, heard their prayer and decided to help. He came to earth in disguise as an old Brahman, wearing white attire. By the time the two brothers opened their eyes, the old man was right in front of them.

"Oh, dear grandpa," said the older brother. "Please help us. We are lost and can't find our way home."

"Well, if you want me to help, you need to answer a riddle first," said the old man.

"What is the riddle, grandpa?" asked the two boys. "We will try our best as this is our only chance."

"Do you see those bamboo clumps?" asked the old man.

"Yes, grandpa," said the two brothers.

"Listen carefully," said the old man.

"There are nine bamboo clumps surrounding you.

"For each clump, there are nine bamboo stems.

"For each bamboo stem, there are nine sections.

"Inside each section, nine bumblebees are singing."

"Yes, grandpa, but what could be your riddle?" asked the boys.

"Tell me how many bumblebees there are in the nine clumps of bamboo," said the old man.

The boys sat down and helped each other think. After a long while, they told the old man the answer.

The old man was very pleased with their answer. "You are very good. Your answer is correct. Now I will take you home, and from now on you will never lack for anything in your life," said the old man.

And so the boys arrived home safely, and they lived happily ever after.

Riddle: What was the boys' answer?

Answer: 6,561 bumblebees.

THE SERVING GIANT

Retold by Pha Sunantha Theerapanyophikkhu, Vientiane, Laos. Collected and retold in English by Wajuppa Tossa.

*O*nce there was a farmer who worked very hard, but he remained poor. One day he was digging the ground to clear the field for the approaching planting season. As he was digging, his hoe hit hard on an object. It was an earthen jar.

"Oh, I am going to be rich. It must be a pot of silver and gold as in the old folktales," thought the farmer.

He hurriedly opened the jar.

Once the jar was opened, smoke came out of it. The farmer became very frightened. He had never heard of smoke coming out of any jar before. He was sitting there waiting to see what would happen.

The smoke began to form, and in a short time there was a huge giant right in front of the farmer.

The man was so frightened that he put his palms together, ready to beg for his life. But the giant bent down to say, "Oh, my dear Master, please don't be afraid of me. I am your servant. I am ready to serve you with whatever you order me to do. Please give me orders now. There is one condition: You must find work for me to do nonstop. Whenever you have nothing more for me to do, I will eat you up."

The farmer was so frightened that he had to think fast to save his life.

"How about if you build me a fully furnished house complete with a beautiful garden?" asked the farmer, thinking that it would take a long time for the giant to pull down the old house, get wood, and begin to build the new house. Thus, he would feel safe.

"Oh, yes, Master, I am at your service right away," said the giant.

But it did not take him more than a few minutes to complete this first order. The giant just put his palms together , made a *wai,* and recited words of incantation, "*Ohm phiang . . . .*"

And there was a beautiful, large wooden house fully furnished with furniture, bedding, kitchen utensils, and everything. Outside there was a splendid flower, vegetable, and herb garden.

"Master, what else do you want me to do?" asked the giant.

Now the farmer had to think quickly. "How about a fruit orchard and rice fields together with a stream running through the land?" asked the farmer. Again, the farmer thought it would surely take the giant a long time to dig up the ground and plant the fruit trees, and rice seedlings. But it did not take the giant more than a few minutes to complete the second order. The giant just put his palms together, made a *wai,* and recited words of incantation, *"Ohm phiang . . . ."* All of a sudden, a beautiful fruit orchard and rice fields were there near the farmer's land. There was even a stream with clear running water that ran alongside the fruit orchard and the rice fields.

"Master, what else do you want me to do? Remember, if you stop telling me to do work, I will eat you up," said the giant.

"How about finding servants to take care of the house and the garden? And workers to work the orchard and the rice fields?" ordered the farmer. Again, the farmer thought it would surely take the giant a long time to find all the people to do housework and field work. But it did not take the giant more than a few minutes to complete the third order. The giant just put his palms together and recited words of incantation, *"Ohm phiang . . . ."* All of a sudden, the house was full of servants and the orchard and rice fields were full of workers, working away diligently.

"Master, what else do you want me to do? Remember, if you stop telling me to do work, I will eat you up," said the giant.

And so the farmer kept ordering the giant to do work nonstop for him. He was still safe as long as he was awake and could give orders. However, as the sun was going down, the farmer became worried. It would be bedtime very soon, as the sun had just gone down. During the daytime, the farmer was not so worried. He could always ask the giant to do this and that, but what would happen during the night? If he fell asleep he would not be able to give orders for the giant to do any work. And that's when the giant would eat him up.

"Master, what else do you want me to do? Remember, if you stop telling me to do work, I will eat you up," said the giant.

What else could he ask the giant to do while he was sleeping? After a long time, the farmer had an idea. He ordered the giant to do one endless job. With that order, he was able to go to sleep restfully. The giant began that job early in the evening of that day. When the farmer woke up, the giant was still working at it. For all I know, the giant may still be doing that job. And the farmer lived happily ever after.

Riddle: What kind of job did the farmer order the giant to do to make him work nonstop?

Pha Sunantha Theerapanyophikkhu's answer: The farmer said, "Now, I would like you to build a round pillar forty meters tall right in front of my house. Then you must climb up to the top of the pillar. Once you are at the top, you must climb down. Then you must climb up again. Do not stop climbing up and down until I give you a new order."

There are many possible answers to this riddle. Students studying children's litera-ture, who had an assignment to read at least four classic young adult novels plus fifty pic-ture books, said, "The farmer ordered the giant to read all the children's classic books." One of the monks in Vientiane said, "The farmer ordered the giant to study, because study-ing would be endless." Answers from other listeners: "The farmer ordered the giant to travel around the universe." "The farmer ordered the giant to guard the house property." "The farmer ordered the giant to sleep." "The farmer ordered the giant not to use magic." "The farmer ordered the giant to show him how to go inside the jar. And then he put the lid back onto the jar." "The farmer ordered the giant to stop using magic and redo everything manually." Can you think of another possible task that would keep the giant busy forever?

THE FATHER'S TEST

Retold by Phra Ajan Xaisomphone Phithiwan (Khen), Vientiane, Laos. Collected and retold in English by Wajuppa Tossa.

A long time ago there was a rich man who had ten sons. He watched his sons grow up with happiness. However, as he was getting older, he began to wonder to whom he would leave his wealth and properties. He had a lot of wealth and properties and would like to leave them to the son who would be able to maintain them for the next generation.

"To whom should I leave my wealth and properties? I don't want my sons to feel that I am partial toward any one of them." He thought about ways to manage this problem day and night. "I must leave my wealth and property to the most virtuous and honest son, but how should I know who is the most virtuous and honest among the ten?" he thought.

Finally, he came up with a plan.

He called his ten sons to see him. Once they were right in front of him, he said, "Sons, you know that I am getting older and older. Very soon I will not be able to manage our wealth and properties. So I will have to test you to see who will inherit the wealth and properties."

The sons listened and wondered what kind of test their father would give them. The rich man continued, "I am giving you these seeds of the yard-long string bean in equal numbers each. You must plant them and take care of them as best you can. After they bear fruit, you can come to show me your job. The one who can grow the most beans with the longest strings will inherit my wealth and properties."

The sons planted the beans, and when the plants had grown they returned to their father.

"Oh, honorable Father, my beans are the longest of all," said the oldest son.

The father laughed with joy when he saw the long string beans.

"Oh, honorable Father, I have the most beans of anyone. Here they are," said the second son.

The father smiled with happiness to see the incredible amount of beans.

"Oh, dear Father, I have the healthiest looking beans here for you," said the third son.

The fourth, fifth, sixth, seventh, eighth, and ninth sons all produced wonderful results. The father praised all of them for their good jobs and said, "Oh, my sons, I am pleased with what you could do. You are diligent and clever. I know that you will be able to take care of yourselves after I am gone."

As everyone was rejoicing over the wonderful produce, the tenth, youngest son came in to see the father, crying.

"Oh, beloved Father, I am so sorry and ashamed of myself. I tried very hard to plant the seeds and took very good care of them, but my seeds just would not sprout."

"I am so sorry that I cannot show you my work as my brothers can. I decided to come and report to you empty handed," explained the youngest son. "Please judge me and do whatever is necessary with me, father."

The father looked at his youngest son with love before saying, "Oh, my son, I give all my wealth and properties to you to manage after I am gone."

The youngest son listened with disbelief. "How can you give me the wealth and properties when I cannot complete the mission that you gave, Father?"

So the father explained. After listening to the father's explanation, all the sons agreed that the youngest son was the most deserving of his father's inheritance. And so they all lived happily ever after.

Riddle: What explanation did the father give for leaving his youngest son the wealth and property?

Answer: The father explained that he had boiled the bean seeds before he gave them to his sons to plant. So the seeds would naturally not sprout. The rich man admired the nine sons' cleverness and their willingness to please him by doing everything to show the healthiest, longest, and most plentiful beans even though the seeds he gave them could not grow. They would be able to survive on their own without any need for the father's wealth and properties. The youngest son was the most virtuous and honest person. The rich man believed that the youngest son would be able to manage and maintain the wealth and property for the longest time.

HUMAN'S AGE

Retold by Pha Sunantha Theerapanyophikku, Vientiane, Laos. Collected and retold in English by Wajuppa Tossa.

*O*nce, long ago, when the world was newly created, Phya Thaen, the highest god in Lao tradition, realized that he did had not given an age limit to humans and some of the animals. So he called Human, Buffalo, Dog, and Monkey to a meeting in heaven.

Once they had arrived, he said, "Now, as I have not given you your ages, I would like to do so today."

"Yes, My Lord," said all the creatures in unison.

"Now Human, your age limit on earth will be thirty years," said Phya Thaen.

"Oh, thank you, My Lord," said the human.

"As for Buffalo, your duty is to help Human work. So you should have the same number of years to live. I will give you a thirty years' limit as well," said Thaen.

"Oh, thank you kindly, Your Majesty, but if I have to help Human work . . . that is very tiring. I would rather stay for only ten years on earth. That's plenty for me," said Buffalo.

"Granted," said Phya Thaen.

The human was listening to all this with glee. The nature of the human is greediness. Thus, he saw the chance of gaining more time on earth.

"Your Majesty, if Buffalo does not want to use his quota of time on earth, I would like to have the number of years that he does not want," said the human.

"Granted," said Phya Thaen.

"Now let's look at Dog. Dog, you were born to help be on guard during the night when the humans are sleeping. You will be forever awake during the night. I will give you thirty years as well," said Phya Thaen.

"Oh, Your Majesty. If I have to stay awake every night . . . that will be very tiring for me. I think ten years would be plenty. Could I just have ten, please?"

"Granted," said Phya Thaen.

Again, the human's greed overtook him, so he said, "Your Majesty, Dog does not want to use his quota of time on earth. I would like to have the number of years that he does not want."

"Granted," said Phya Thaen.

"Now let's consider Monkey's age. I sent you to be born on earth to entertain the humans after their hard work. You must be able to make them laugh. So I will give you also thirty years," said Phya Thaen.

"Oh, Your Majesty. It might be very difficult to make humans laugh all the time. I don't think I could keep that up for thirty years. Could I please just have ten years, like Dog and Buffalo?"

"Granted," said Phya Thaen

The human's greed took control of him again. So he said, "Your Majesty, if Monkey does not want to use his quota of time on earth, I would like to have the number of years to add to my original age."

"Granted," said Phya Thaen.

Then Phya Thaen made his final proclamation: "From now on Buffalo, Dog, and Monkey will each have ten years on earth. Human will have his original thirty plus twenty from Buffalo, twenty from Dog, and twenty from Monkey."

Riddle: First, what is the maximum age of the human on earth? Second, how do the years he got from Buffalo, Dog, and Monkey affect Human?

Answers: (1) The human could live to be ninety years old. (2) Lao tradition holds that human characteristics change in three stages. For the first thirty years of life, the human behaves like a human being. But at age thirty, the human starts to work very hard. His life is now like that of the buffalo. These are the years he took from the buffalo. Then the human reaches age fifty. Now he begins the years he took from the dog. The human has trouble sleeping and stays awake all night worrying. At last he reaches the age of seventy. Now he is using the years he took from the monkey. He begins to act silly, forget things, and behave like a monkey. His antics now make people laugh. This is how the human uses the years he was given by Phya Thaen and also the years he took from the animals.

PART 7

Ghost Stories

PHI YA WOM: THE GRANDMA GHOST NAMED WOM

From "Phi Ya Wom," by Somsaeng Kesawila, in *Hom Nithan Phuen Muen*. Retold by Wajuppa Tossa.

*O*nce, long ago, when the earth and sky were so close that anyone could stretch up and reach the sky from earth easily, and the mountains were only as tall as the rice plants, a grandma ghost called Phi Ya Wom lived in the forest near the town of Muangtai Muangtang. Her foods were animals, and people who happened to wander into the forest.

One day two orphan sisters wandered into the forest in Grandma Wom's territory. Grandma Wom haunted them in various ghostly forms, laughing and saying: "Who sent you to invade my forest? Ha, ha, ha!" Then she recited this verse:

Yuu taam yuu sin laen maa haa	I live here; by and by my meat speeds to me
Paa laen maa suu	and hurriedly comes my fish.
Yuu taam yuu bun paak haak mii	I live here; by and by my mouth will be blessed with food
Khong kin dii maen song oey nong	and my tasty food is this good pair of sisters.

"Ha, ha, ha! I will preserve you two to feed my children."

The older sister kept very calm, holding her little sister in her arms, speaking sweetly to Grandma Wom: "We are orphans. Each day, we wander into hills and forests to dig up roots for our food, as we have no good rice to eat. Grandma Wom, the queen of this forest, who is blessed with meat, fish, and rice, please have mercy on us and let us go alive."

Grandma Wom, hearing this, pretended to be kind. She saw that she could use these two sisters as her bait to get more people to eat.

"Oh, dear children, I didn't know that you were orphans. I feel sorry for you; I will let you go. Before you go, I will give you some food. Since I don't have fish and meat, I can give you some sugarcane. Eat this and remember:

Mue laan yaang kap baan	When you walk home,
Hen thaang piik hai cao mai	if you see a merging road, you must make a mark;
Yam khii oy khaai pa	When you chew on the sugarcane, spit out the residue;
Yam thaang pen hoi wai	step on the path repeatedly to leave a trace
Yam laan com lue ceb khai	When you are down or sick
Yaa ca pai yaam wae	Grandma will visit you
Mii yang dae yaak dai	Whatever you would wish to have
Yaam nan haak si ao mue ton de	Grandma will collect them for you later.

The two sisters did as they were told. They marked their trail just as she had told them. Grandma Wom followed the girls' tracks of sugarcane residue and the worn and trodden paths they took. Then she attacked the people, until no one was left except the two sisters, who tried to escape the best they could. The two sisters ran to their house and pulled up the ladder as Grandma Wom approached the house.

Grandma Wom arrived at the house and found there was no ladder to climb. So she called, "Dear Grandchildren, how can I get into the house? There is no ladder."

The younger sister said, "Oh, Grandma, we never had a ladder."

"How did you go up into the house without a ladder?" she asked the girls.

"We climbed up backward. If you want to come up, please climb up backward."

So Grandma Wom did. The two sisters pushed her back down with whatever was near, the firewood, the spade, and so on.

Then Grandma Wom had to go to the toilet, so she called to the two sisters, "Please help, I have to go badly."

The two sisters said, "We have no toilet here. You must run to the outhouse near the water hole." So Grandma Wom did. While she was gone, the two sisters ran to the tallest tree of bael fruit and climbed to the top.

Grandma Wom came back to the house and found no one. So she followed their smell until she came under the tree. She looked up and asked the two sisters to drop a ladder for her to follow them. The two sisters said, "We have no ladder here."

"How did you climb the tree, then?"

"We climbed up the tree trunk backward. If you want to come up, you have to climb up backward, too," replied the sisters.

So she did. As she was climbing backward, the girls pushed her down with twigs, bael fruit, and whatever else was near.

Then Grandma Wom had to go to the toilet again. She called to the two sisters, "Please help, I have to go badly."

The two sisters said, "We have no toilet up here. You must run to the forest near the mountains."

So Grandma Wom did. While she was gone, the two sisters ran to the tree with more bael fruit and climbed to the top.

Then Grandma Wom returned to the fruit tree and did not see the sisters. So she followed them to the right tree.

This kept happening over and over. Every time Grandma Wom would go off to use the toilet, the sisters would climb down and run to another bael tree. But every time Grandma Wom would find them again. The sisters were just running out of baal trees to climb when the little sister looked up in the sky and saw her parents washing dishes in heaven.

"Mama, Papa, please drop a rope for us to climb up to you," she begged .

"We can't right now," replied her parents. "We are preparing our knives and tools to clear our fields."

"Mama and Papa, PLEASE drop a rope for us!"

But her parents replied. "We can't right now. We are busy clearing our fields."

The next time the little girl called, they said "We are busy burning weeds in our fields."

And then, "We are busy planting our cotton plants now."

"Oh PLEASE!" called the older sister. "Please drop the rope to us quickly. Grandma Wom is tearing up the bael tree and will eat us for her food."

This time the parents replied, "Planting cotton plants, we get cotton. Spinning cotton, we get thread. Braiding the thread, we get a rope. Now we can drop the rope down."

After a long time, the rope was slowly dropped down. The little sister went up first. Then the rope was dropped down again for the older sister. As she was grabbing the rope, Grandma Wom came and jumped up to try to grasp the rope, but she was too late. The rope was pulled up. All Grandma Wom could grab was the soles of the older sister's feet.

The two sisters were safe, but not really. Grandma Wom tricked the girls' parents by transforming herself into a human, crying and moaning, begging the girls' parents to drop the rope down for her. The father thought she was a human, so he dropped down the rope, not listening to his daughters. Then he began to pull up the rope, with Grandma Wom in human form hanging onto it.

"Father, please do not pull up Grandma Wom. She will come and eat all of us and all of the celestial beings in heaven," the girls pleaded. But the father did not listen; he continued pulling the rope up and up.

The older sister, feeling certain that her father would not stop pulling up the rope, cut the rope before Grandma Wom could reach heaven.

Grandma Wom's body fell down so hard on the mountains that it made a great crater filled with water, which became Wang Ya Wom (Grandma Wom's Whirlpool). The redwood trees and their kind, the white gooseberries, and the palm trees were crushed to extinction. Grandma Wom's body was broken into millions of pieces all over the place. These pieces of Grandma Wom became mosquitoes, bed bugs, wasps, bees, hornets, centipedes, snakes, and dangerous creatures with sharp claws and teeth. To this day, these creatures still follow human beings, trying to bite them. The soles of the feet of the older sister that were grabbed by Grandma Wom gave all human beings the arches of the feet from that day until now.

PHI KONGKOI: THE GHOST NAMED KONGKOI

Told by Suphaphit Khantha, Mahasarakham, Thailand. Collected and retold in English by Wajuppa Tossa.

*O*nce there was a man named Thid Kaew who lived with his old mother. Thid Kaew was a grateful son who took very good care of his mother. He earned a living by fishing. At first he could get a lot of fish, but later there was no fish, not a single fish. So he went to tell his mother about this.

"There must be someone stealing our fish. Why don't you go and watch the trap?" suggested his mother.

So Thid Kaew went to hide near his fish trap. Later that night he saw a dark shadow emerging from a bush, shrieking, "*Kok kok kok Koi koi koi.*" It was Phi Kongkoi, the female ghost named Kongkoi.

Thid Kaew jumped on the shadow, and it cried, "*Kok kok kok Koi koi koi,* (Hungry! Hungry!)." Thid Kaew wrestled the shadow down, and they struggled for a long time. Finally he subdued the hungry ghost. Now she looked beautiful to him. So he became the husband of Phi Kongkoi. He was very happy.

As the golden rays of the sun appeared in the sky at dawn, the rooster crowed, "Egg-i-en-egg." Thid Kaew woke up. He stretched, but . . . whoops! He almost fell off the high branch of a tree. "Oh, no. How did I get up here?" he asked himself. He called out:

"Help! Help! Thid Kaew can climb up the tree, but not down. Help! Help! Thid Kaew can climb up the tree, but not down."

It was cool in the morning, but Thid Kaew was drenched with sweat. Nobody came to help. Thid Kaew tried to climb down, with difficulty, and finally he managed to get down from the tree. Once his feet touched the ground, he began running, running, running.

He was running around and around in the forest until dark. He came across a little hut in the field. There he saw Phi Kongkoi, crying, saying, "Oh, dear husband, we can't live together. I have to go my way. But before I go away, I will give you some treasures that I have." Then she handed the treasures to Thid Kaew, and Phi Kongkoi disappeared.

Thid Kaew grabbed the treasures and ran back home to his mother. It was real treasure. And the ghost lady was really gone forever. So they lived happily ever after.

PHI KHON LONG: THE GHOST WHO CARRIED HER OWN COFFIN

Told by Bounyok Saensounthone, Vientiane, Laos. Collected and retold in English by Wajuppa Tossa.

Many Lao women are excellent weavers. They grow cotton or raise silkworms, spin the thread, and weave beautiful cloth. In this story the young man is taking some of his family's woven goods to market to sell.

*O*nce, long ago, in a village near the Mekong River, there lived a beautiful girl. Her parents had died while she was growing up, so she lived by herself in a small wooden house on the riverbank. Farther down the riverbank lived her handsome boyfriend and his family. Everyone in the village admired these young lovers. They felt that the girl and her boyfriend were made for one another. Every day the boy would visit her and they would enjoy being together.

One day the boy came to visit the girl and told her that he had to go away.

"My beloved, I have to go away to sell some silk and cotton cloth from my family," said the boy.

"Oh, no, you are going to be away from me! How can I go on living without you?" said the girl sadly.

"When I return, my parents promise to arrange our wedding ceremony for us," said the boy.

"Is that true?" asked the girl.

"Yes, my parents said I need to make enough money so that we could build our own family," explained the boy.

"All right, I will wait for you no matter what happens," vowed the girl.

The boy left the next day, rowing his boat upstream to sell his cloth in faraway cities. The girl remained in her house alone. Every day people would see her sitting on the steps on the river bank, looking upstream, waiting for her boyfriend's return.

Time went by, but the boy was still away and the girl became paler and sickly looking. One day she was seen sitting on the river bank coughing.

"What happened to you, girl? Are you not feeling well? You should not be sitting in the strong wind like that. You will get really sick," warned one of the older ladies in the village.

"Oh, I am all right. I just want to be the first one my boyfriend sees when he returns from his trip," answered the girl hopefully.

"Take care of yourself," said the elderly woman as she walked away.

A year went by very quickly for everyone, but not for the girl. By the end of the year, no one saw her sitting on the steps any more. Her house was completely dark at night. The older people in the village noticed the change and decided to break into her house one day. When they went inside the dark house, they could smell a strong odor whiffing through the air. They looked around the house, and saw the girl's lifeless body on the floor.

They lit a large candle, made her a wooden coffin, and lifted her body into place in the coffin. They left the house to tell everybody to come and help prepare the funeral. Some went to invite the monks to come and perform Buddhist religious rites for the deceased. The girl in her coffin was left all alone in the dim, deserted house.

Late that night people heard sounds coming from the house, but no one dared go and see, except a group of teenagers. They became very curious about what could be happening in that house. So they challenged each other to go and see.

"Now, I bet you don't dare go to see what makes noise in that house," challenged one boy to the others.

"Oh, I can go if I want to. Do you want to bet?" one of the boys answered the challenge.

"Yes, I can bet with you. If you go near there and peek in, I will do all the work in the field for you and your parents," said the first boy.

"Deal," said the second boy.

The other boys waited quite far away from the house, and the boy who had accepted the challenge slowly and gingerly walked toward the dim house. He approached the house and saw a crack in the wall. So he peeked in. What he saw petrified him. He could not say a word or move away from that spot. He just stood there with his eyes wide open.

The other boys began to wonder, so they walked closer. They saw the first boy standing there, so they thought there was nothing scary. They went to him and pushed him away from the crack and looked through it. Each of the boys who saw inside became paralyzed.

They saw a woman carrying a coffin on her shoulder, walking around the room! When she turned facing them, they saw that her face was disintegrated and distorted and her body was covered with maggots all over.

The next day, the news spread through the village. The dead girl now became known by the name *phi khon long* (a ghost who carries her coffin). After that day, nobody dared to go near the house. The sounds continued every single night from that house.

Not long after that, the boy returned to the village, rowing his boat closest to his girl-friend's house. He rowed fast, as he missed his girlfriend very much and wished to be with her as soon as possible. By the time he approached the girl's house, it was dusk. When he got closer, he saw his girlfriend sitting on the steps, waiting for him. She was smiling happily. He stopped his boat and climbed up to the steps where she was waiting for him.

"Oh, I am so happy you returned as you promised," she said.

"Yes, I made a lot of money. We can be married soon," said the boy.

"Oh, please come to have some dinner. I can prepare it for you," she said.

"Yes, I am so hungry. I can eat anything now," said the boy.

So he went into the house and the tray of food was ready for him. He sat down and ate. Once he finished eating, she invited him to stay for a visit before going home. But the boy excused himself, saying that he had to go tell his parents that he was back. He was afraid that they would be worried about him.

"All right. You may go home, but please come right back tonight. We need to catch up on a lot of things," said the girl.

The boy boarded his boat and rowed home very fast. He wanted to meet his parents and then return to his girlfriend right away.

At home, his parents were very happy to see him. But when he said he would go to visit his girlfriend, they were horrified.

"Oh, no, you cannot go to visit her. She has become a ghost carrying a coffin. She died a year after you left," explained the parents.

The boy became very angry and replied, "Oh, no, Father, Mother, I cannot believe you. She is alive. I had dinner with her before I came home."

"Oh, no, you ate the food of the ghost! That's not good. You must not return to her, my son," the parents said in alarm.

The boy could control his temper no longer. He shouted, "I don't believe you. You don't want me to marry her. That's why you keep saying all this nonsense. I am going to see her now." With that he ran out of the house and ran directly to the girl's house.

"Oh, my dear, you returned. I am so delighted," said the girl in ecstasy. "Please come up so we can talk."

They talked about this and that as if they had never been parted. Not long after that the boy became sleepy. And the girl said, "Oh, why don't you sleep here with me tonight? We are going to be married soon anyway. You can go home tomorrow morning."

"Well, actually, it's a good idea," said the boy, as the girl prepared the bedding for him to sleep on.

Part 7: Ghost Stories

They lay down side by side. The boy was so sleepy that he began to doze off. But while he was sleeping, he heard some gnawing sounds. So he asked her without opening his eyes, "Oh, my dear, what is that noise?"

"Oh, *khob men, khob men, khob men*. (This could mean, "I am biting some bed bugs" or "I am getting rid of the bed bugs".) Don't worry, please go to sleep," answered the girl.

The boy fell asleep again, but not long after that he woke up because he heard louder biting sounds beside him. So he asked without opening his eyes, "What is that sound, dear?"

The girl answered in a shrill voice, *"Khob non, khob non, khob non*. (This could mean "I am biting a maggot" or "I am sleeping. Please go ahead and sleep".)

The boy fell asleep again, but the sound did not stop. He opened the corners of his eyes to see the girl. And to his great fear, he saw the girl's decayed body with maggots crawling around her. She was picking off the maggots and biting them. This time he recalled his parents' warning. "The girl is dead."

What could he do? He had to think fast and get out of her house as soon as possible, but how?

"Oh, my dear, I need to go to the toilet now," he said.

"Oh, you don't have to go to the outhouse. You could just do it on the veranda. I will tie the rope around your waist to prevent you from falling off the veranda," said the girl, tying the boy's waist with one end of a rope and holding onto the other end.

The boy got out of bed and went to stand on the veranda, thinking quickly what to do next. He loosened the rope around his waist slightly and pulled it up and over his head. He tied it around the water jar on the veranda and poked a small hole in the side of the jar. It sounded like he was urinating. Then he hurried down the stairs and quickly ran toward his home. He ran as fast as his feet could carry him. But halfway there, he heard the girl's shrill voice not too far behind him, "Where are you going? Please come back."

At that point he almost ran into a tall palm tree. He quickly climbed up the palm tree. When the ghost was under the tree, she called him, "Please come down now and let's go home."

The boy picked one palm fruit and said, "Now you must catch me. I am jumping down now." He threw the palm fruit down far from the foot of the tree, and the ghost ran to catch it in her hands. Once she realized that it was just a palm fruit, she called him, "Oh, darling, please come down now."

This time the man saw a family of civet cats. He picked up one baby and said, "Now, I am really jumping down, watch, and catch."

He threw the baby civet cat back toward the girl's house as far as he could. "Here I come," he shouted.

The ghost ran back quite far from the tree. She caught the baby civet cat in her arms and cried, "Oh, no, you have been turned into a baby civet cat," she cried and wailed.

Then the boy climbed down as fast as he could and ran home. By the time he got to his house, the ghost was right in front of the house.

"You are not turned into a civet cat. You can't fool me. Please come home with me," begged the ghost.

"Oh, my dear, you are dead. You must not bother me any more. We are in a different world now," said the boy.

"We can still live together," said the ghost.

"Oh, you live in the world of the dead now. You must go to be reborn. You cannot be together with a human like my son," said the father.

"No, give me back my husband now," commanded the ghost.

"No, I will not give my son to a ghost. Go away," said the father firmly.

The ghost cried and moaned painfully. "Please give me my husband. I will do anything for you."

"You will?" asked the father.

"Yes, anything! If only I can have my husband back," promised the ghost.

"All right," said the father, throwing his fishing net at the ghost.

"Here, count the holes in the fishing net. When you have the right number, I will give my son back to you."

"All right!" said the ghost, beginning to count. "One, two, three, . . . three hundred . . . . Oh no, I missed one hole here. I have to begin counting again. One, two, three, . . . four hundred . . . ."

The ghost kept counting and counting and counting until the first ray of the sun appeared in the sky. Her voice became weaker and weaker and her body began to lose its shape. By the time dawn came, she had disappeared.

The next day, the boy and his family went to offer food to the monks and transferred the merit to comfort the girl's spirit. From that day on, the girl never reappeared or made the sound of walking and carrying a coffin again.

Since then, it is believed that one should keep a fishing net within reach at the front of every house. Then if any ghost comes to haunt you, you can simply throw a fishing net for the ghost to count.

PHI KHAO PUN: THE NOODLE SELLER GHOST

Told by Natthakan Photjanaphimon, Nongkhai, Thailand. Collected and retold in English by Wajuppa Tossa.

*T*here was a man who earned a living by selling *khao pun,* or rice noodles with condiments and vegetables. He would put his noodles on the back of his *xaleng* tricycle and go around the area to sell them.

One day he went to sell his noodles as usual. It was getting late, but he had not sold all of his noodles yet. He decided to go to a village where he had never been before. As he was approaching the village, the road diverged into two paths. On the side of the road were twin huge banyan trees with thick branches bending toward each other. They created a large shady area. As he was driving past, he saw a young woman standing under the trees. So he stopped and offered her a ride. The girl sat looking down, with her hair covering her face.

At that time it was dusk, and it was getting darker and darker. The man felt a strange sense of chill. He thought he could strike up a conversation because it was getting quiet and eerie.

He said, "My younger sister, do you live in this village?"

The girl kept her face down, not saying anything.

He continued, "Are you coming to visit your relatives in this village?"

The girl kept her face down, not saying anything.

He continued, "Don't you think it is unusually chilly today?"

The girl kept her face down, not saying anything.

He continued, "Is it true what they said, that there are a lot of fierce ghosts around here?"

The girl kept her face down, not saying anything.

He continued, "Standing there by yourself, aren't you afraid?"

The girl kept her face down, not saying anything.

He continued, "Are you a human? If not, are you a ghost?"

The girl looked up and nodded her head a few times.

The brave *khao pun* vendor asked, "How did you become a ghost? Who harmed you?"

The girl looked right at him and shouted, "A noodle seller like YOU!"

The next day, people in the village reported that they saw noodles scattered under the shade of the twin banyan trees. The villagers knew that someone had been haunted by the ghostly noodle seller girl again. It was said that the girl ghost was a *khao pun* vender as well. She had been murdered under the twin banyan trees, and her body was buried there.

PART 8

Tales of Magic and Elaborate Tales

SANG SINXAI

Retold by Kongdeuane Nettavong. Translated by Wajuppa Tossa.

Lao tales contain many magical elements. This story features a magical flying giant!

Once, a long time ago, there was a city called Pengjan, whose ruler was Phaya Kutsalad. Phya Kutsalad's queen was Nang Jantha. The king had a sister named Nang Sumuntha.

One day Nang Sumuntha and her servants went to visit the royal garden outside of the palace. While she was enjoying the flowers in the garden, a magical giant happened to soar by, looking for an animal to feast on. This was the giant king, Khumphan, from the giants' city called Anolahd. He saw Nang Sumuntha and fell in love with her. He descended from the sky to swoop up Nang Sumuntha and soared away to his own city.

When Phya Kutsalad, the king of Pengjan, learned this news, he was so miserable that he could not eat or sleep. He kept thinking about his younger sister. As a result, he renounced the throne to go in search of his sister. He became ordained as a holy man and went traveling through the forest. Arriving at a city called Jampa, he went out to take alms early in the morning as usual. There he saw a rich man's seven beautiful sisters offering food to the monks. When it was his turn to receive food from the sisters, he saw that they were very beautiful. He fell in love with all seven of these beautiful sisters! He could not remain a monk with these feelings. So he left the monkhood and returned to his city.

Now that he had become a king again, Phya Kutsalad sent his ministers to ask for the hands of these seven sisters in marriage, according to customary rite. He thought also, that if the sisters bore sons, those sons could help search for his stolen sister.

Not long after that, his queen, Nang Jantha, and his seven wives all became pregnant. After nine months, they bore babies. However, Nang Jantha had an elephant as her son. And the youngest of the seven wives had twins, a conch shell boy and a boy who was born with a bow and arrows in his hands. The six other wives had a son each. However, they were jealous of Nang Jantha and their youngest sister for having special and unique sons. So they decided to get rid of them. They bribed the court astrologer to say that the three sons would bring disaster if they were allowed to remain in the city. The king believed this prediction and sent the two wives and their sons away.

The two wives and their children wandered aimlessly into the deep and dark forest. They suffered a great deal on this dangerous journey. Phya In of heaven looked down and found that the two wives and the sons were suffering. He decided to conjure up a castle in the middle of the forest for them to stay in. He named the elephant son Siho and the conch shell son Sangthong. The other son was named Sinxai. The wives and three sons lived happily in the forest castle built for them by Phya In.

As for the six other sons of the king, they grew up to become six handsome young men. They led carefree lives in the palace. The king ordered them to go learn knowledge of magical powers from able masters. However, the sons did not pay much attention to their studies. When they returned home, the father assumed they had learned everything. So he sent them in search of their aunt, Nang Sumuntha.

After receiving this order, the six sons began their journey in the forest aimlessly. Finally they got lost and wandered into the castle of their brothers and stepmothers. The six sons realized who the people were right away. So they claimed to bring an order from the king for Siho, Sangthong, and Sinxai to go search for their stolen aunt. The stepmothers and their three sons easily fell into the trap of the six scheming sons. Sangthong, Sinxai, and Siho asked the six sons to take care of their mothers and then went on their way to search for Nang Sumuntha.

The three brave brothers traveled, meeting and conquering enemies on their way. Finally they reached Anolahd City, where they conquered the giant Khumphan and brought their aunt back. The six brothers wanted to take Nang Sumuntha to present to the king, without bringing Siho, Sangthong, and Sinxai along. So when they reached the city gate, the six brothers told Siho, Sangthong, and Sinxai to purify themselves before entering the city by taking a wash at the cliffside. Then, as Siho, Sangthong, and Sinxai were bathing there, the six brothers came and pushed them off the cliff.

Then six brothers told their aunt that Siho, Sangthong, and Sinxai had drowned at the cliff edge. Nang Sumuntha did not believe them. She ran to find the bodies of Siho, Sangthong, and Sinxai, and realized that they had been murdered by the wicked brothers. She put a few of her belongings in Sinxai's hands as a sign of thanks and of her good memories for him. Then she went to the city with the six brothers.

Once the aunt and the six brothers arrived at the city, Nang Sumuntha told the king that the six brothers had caused the deaths of Siho, Sangthong, and Sinxai. The king was infuriated by such news. He sent the six sons, their mothers, and the court astrologer into exile.

Meanwhile, Phya In had seen all that was going on and did not want to leave things this way. So he came down to bring Sinxai's life back to him and took him to the castle to live with his mother. Phya In was not able to bring Sangthong and Siho back to life, as their time on earth had expired.

The king now took a royal procession to bring his two wives and son back to live in the city. And they lived happily ever after. He apologized to the two wives and relinquished the throne to Sinxai, and the story ended happily.

THAO KHANGKHAM, THE CHAMELEON PRINCE

Told by Khamsing Wongsawang, National Libraries, Vientiane, Laos. Translated by Wajuppa Tossa.

*O*nce, a long time ago, there was a beautiful maiden who lived in a village. She was never married, but one day she became pregnant. The village headman thought it was not right that a young unmarried maiden should be pregnant. He interrogated her, but she said she had never had a relationship with any man. All she did was eat a strange fruit one day when she went to the forest to gather some forest food. No one believed her. She was then sent to the king for judgment.

The king also agreed that it was not proper for an unmarried maiden to be pregnant. She had to be beheaded. But as she was carrying a child in her womb, the king allowed her to wait until she bore the baby. Then the baby would tell who its father was.

Not long after that, the woman delivered, not a baby, but a golden chameleon who could speak human language. It was so strange that the king forgot about his order to behead her. So she lived in a little hut in the royal garden near the palace with her golden chameleon son, named Thao Khangkham. At about the same time as the chameleon was born, the king also had seven girls. They grew up to be beautiful princesses.

One day the king planned to take his seven daughters to visit the flower garden. When Thao Khangkham heard about this, he asked his mother's permission to go to the garden to look at the daughters of the king. In spite of his mother's objections, Thao Khangkham went to perch on a tree near the flower garden. The princesses were sitting under the tree. Thao Khangkham teased one of the princesses by touching her cheeks with his tail, but she could not see who did it.

After a while, the king and his six daughters returned to the palace, but the youngest princess decided to stay on a little longer. Thao Khangkham told her that she was now his fiancée. He would tell his mother to go ask for her hand from the king.

After that day, Thao Khangkham asked his mother to have the village headman take her to the palace so she could ask for the youngest princess's hand in marriage. The mother

---

had only one bunch of bananas to take as a gift, but she went to the palace as her chameleon son requested. The king was annoyed by such a simple gift and such a strange request, but he could not punish her in any way; there was not a law in the ancient ruling system to punish a person who brought only bananas to ask for a hand in marriage. So he challenged her to build a silver and gold bridge with elaborate peacock designs from her hut to the palace. If she could do that, Thao Khangkham could marry the king's youngest daughter. But if she could not do that, she would be sentenced to death.

The mother was upset and afraid, but she came back to tell her son about it anyway. Thao Khangkham said there was no problem. He could bring the "father and mother" of silver and gold to build the bridge, but only if the villagers would help him. All the villagers thought it was so curious that they decided to help him; they wanted to see what the "father and mother" of silver and gold were like.

Thao Khangkham instructed them to walk in the forest and to bring baskets with them. They had to clear away all the trees for three or four days. After four days, he told them to set the baskets as traps and to catch whatever flew into the baskets. Then they had to take them home. When they reached the village, they had to dig a hole six meters wide, ten meters long, and six meters deep to hold the "father and mother" of silver and gold.

The villagers went and did everything according to Thao Khangkham's instructions. Now that the "father and mother" of silver and gold were held in their village, they could access all the gold and silver they needed. So Thao Khangkham ordered the villagers to build the bridge with silver and gold crossbeams. Once it was done, he needed to have the elaborate peacock designs carved on the bridge. However, none of the villagers was skilled in making such designs. So he made a wish to the celestial beings to inspire artists to come by his village. Sure enough, artists arrived. They decorated the bridge as he asked. Not long after that the bridge was splendidly completed.

Then Thao Khangkham gathered all the villagers to go to the palace in a great procession. There was nothing the king could do at this point. So he agreed to have his youngest daughter marry Thao Khangkham. But they had to go build their own dwelling place outside the palace.

Once they were in their little hut, the golden chameleon told the princess, "Now as you can see, I am only a chameleon. If you love me, you can live with me, but if not, I understand. If a handsome young man happens by, you could marry him."

Not long after that, a handsome young man came to visit the princess at the hut. She was civil with the young man, but she could not go with him, as she was married to the golden chameleon. The handsome young man came almost every day, but she refused to leave with him. She told him that she was already married. But she noticed that every time the young man came, the chameleon was not home. One day, when the handsome young man was visiting, she happened to see the skin of the chameleon at one corner of the hut. By now she was sure that the handsome young man was really her chameleon husband. "He has come out of his skin," she thought. "But he will not go back into it again!" So she grabbed the chameleon skin and threw it into the fire.

"Oh, no, why did you do that?" asked the young man. "That chameleon skin was my magical power. I could have built us a castle with that power."

"That's all right. I don't need the magical power here and now. I just want to live with you as a normal husband and wife. That's all," said the princess.

And so they lived happily ever after, until one day a powerful enemy army attacked the princess's father's city. Nobody could conquer the enemy. The king sent word to the princess to get help.

Once Thao Khangkham heard this, he went to confront the enemy right away. He fought with the entire army by himself and chased them away.

The king was very impressed with the handsome young man's extraordinary power. He told him and his wife to return to the city. Once they were in the city, the princess reported to the king everything that had happened to them. The king was even more impressed, and he was overjoyed for his youngest daughter. He decided to relinquish the throne and let Thao Khangkham become king. And so the entire city lived happily ever after.

THAO CHET HAI

Retold by Wajuppa Tossa.

*I*n a village near Thotsaraj city, there was a poor couple who had been married for a long time, but they never had a child to help them work. Many years went by, and they grew older and older. When they were very old, the wife became pregnant. She was big with child for three years without any sign of going into labor. The husband could not go anywhere for fear that his wife would be in labor while he was gone. But after three years he could no longer wait, as they had become poorer and poorer. So one day he told his wife that he would like to make a boat and go to do some trading. His wife told him not to worry about her; she was sure that the baby would not come while her husband was gone. Or, if the baby came, she would be able to manage. So the husband prepared his tools and went out to make a boat for himself in the forest.

Not long after the husband had gone out to make his boat, the wife went into labor. All her relatives came to lend a helping hand. After a long time, the baby was born. He fell down, broke the floor, fell right through the floor onto the water buffalo that was tied under the house, and broke the water buffalo's neck. When the wind touched the baby's body, he grew huge. Then he ran to the river to clean himself up and ran home. The entire village became frightened of this boy who became a full-grown man in one day. Some young girls, seeing the newborn naked baby-man, were embarrassed. The boy-man went home and frightened away all the relatives who had come to help with the birth. The boy stepped up to the house, and he was as tall as the ceiling. His mother found the largest piece of cloth she had for him to wear. Then the boy said he was hungry. So she gave him the entire pot of sticky rice and a jar full of meat. He ate it but was not full; he kept asking for more and more. His mother called him Thao Chet Hai (The Seven Jars), because he ate seven huge jars of food at a time. After he was satisfied, he asked for his father. His mother pointed the way to the forest where the old man was cutting trees to make a boat.

Once the boy got to the forest, he could see an old man cutting down a huge tree. He knew that the old man was his father. So he told the man to fell the tree and he would carry it home. The old man was tired and perturbed, thinking that someone was challenging him. So he cut down the huge tree, but as it fell the boy caught it. Then they returned home. The parents as well as the villagers were so afraid of the boy-man that they suggested the old couple send the boy away from the village.

One day the father said to Thao Chet Hai: "Chet Hai, my son, you must go to collect debts from a giant couple in the faraway land in the south. The giant is called Li Puu Laa Nam. He and his wife borrowed our money and treasures from us long ago and never returned to pay their debts." The boy was more than delighted to take this responsibility. So he set off to find the giants. Then the father and mother became very sad, because they had sent their own son to meet his peril. It was believed that nobody could return from the giant's land alive. In addition to the giants, there were many monsters and demons in that land.

Thao Chet Hai went on his way with no problems. All animals and demons became so scared of him that they fled from his path. On his way, Thao Chet Hai met seven strong friends: Fisherman; Squirrel Catcher, Wind Catcher, Ox Catcher, Elephant Catcher, Water Drinker, and Coral Tree Puller. The eight friends came across a wide river, and there was no boat to cross. So each friend decided to jump over the river, but seven fell and a great fish swallowed them all. Thao Chet Hai was the last to jump. The fish opened its mouth and caught one of his feet, but Thao Chet Hai landed with the fish stuck on his foot. He opened up the fish and found his seven friends all dead inside.

He was feeling hopelessly sad. Suddenly a Grandma Ghost, Ya Wom, who could smell the dead, appeared at the scene where Thao Chet Hai was watching over his seven friends' bodies. She thought she would eat the one that was alive first, as the dead ones would be there for her after she finished the living man. But Thao Chet Hai put up a great fight and defeated her. Ya Wom begged for mercy. She promised to bring back Thao Chet Hai's friends, if he would let her go. So Thao Chet Hai agreed. Ya Wom brought them all back to life. And the eight friends continued their journey to see the giants.

Once they reached the giants' home, the eight friends were given challenges by the giants. First, they were challenged to drink whiskey and stay sober. Second, they were told to fight the giant himself. In both cases, Thao Chet Hai won. He drank the whiskey with no ill effects and was able to slay the giant.

The eight friends cut open the stomach of the dead giant and there they found silver, gold, and other treasures. The giant's wife explained that he had swallowed all the treasure they were guarding, thinking this would make his body so heavy that no one could knock him over. But Thao Chet Hai had proved too strong for the giant.

The eight men then built a ship in which they carried the giant's treasures home. But the wife of the giant shouted a curse after them, cursing them to die like her husband.

Once home they went to Thao Chet Hai's parents and gave treasures to them and to other people in the village. Everybody but the eight strong men lived happily. Each felt lonely and would like to have a wife. But they realized that they could not marry human beings because they were too strong for any human beings. They decided to go to heaven to ask for the daughters of the head of the celestial beings, Phya Thaen. After they built a bridge from earth to heaven, they began climbing up. But the bridge collapsed. The female giant's curse came true. All of them died from broken necks.

The villagers organized a cremation for the eight men, but their bodies would not burn. So the villagers built replicas of the eight daughters of Phya Thaen and held a wedding ceremony for the dead heroes. Then their bodies could be cremated and their spirits were satisfied. And thus ends the story of Thao Chet Hai.

SEVEN FRIENDS

Told by Somboon Thana-ouan, Mahasarakham, Thailand. Collected and retold in English by Wajuppa Tossa.

*O*nce, long ago, the king of Pharanasii had seven daughters. He ruled the city peaceably. But one day a wild ox came to attack the city. The wild ox began to harm people daily. The king issued a proclamation: "If anyone can defeat this wild ox, I will give my seven daughters as a reward."

At that time there were seven friends who came to volunteer to fight the wild ox. The seven friends grabbed their lances and sabers, intending to destroy the wild ox. Then they went out to confront the ox. But when the ox appeared, they became so frightened that they all ran to hide in a hollow log.

The wild ox charged at the seven men at great speed with its mouth open. When it got to the log, it swallowed the entire log with the seven men carrying their lances and sabers inside, as easily as if it were swallowing a banana tree trunk.

The seven men inside the wild ox stomach discussed how they could survive and agreed that they would chop the inside of the log and build a fire. So they did.

Now the wild ox's stomach became unbearably hot, because:

Kong fai mai. (The firewood is burning.)

Phai nai sum chuud. (The inside of his stomach is painfully burned.)

There was a burning fire inside the ox's stomach. So he ran to the swamp, writhing with pain and suffering. Not long after that he died.

Now there was a very little carp called *pa siew* who came across this wild ox. So he swallowed the wild ox. The wild ox, the log, the seven men, and the burning fire were now inside the little carp stomach. And again:

Kong fai mai. (The firewood is burning.)

Phai nai sum chuud. (The inside of his stomach is painfully burned.)

The burning fire was inside the carp's stomach. So that little carp writhed with pain and suffering. Not long after that he died.

Now there was a small kingfisher, *nok ten*, flying to alight at the ogress's fish trap. He saw the little fish floating in the water. So he swallowed the little carp. Now the little carp, the wild ox, the log, the seven men, and the burning fire were inside the small kingfisher's stomach. And again:

Kong fai mai. (The firewood is burning.)

Phai nai sum chuud. (The inside of his stomach is painfully burned.)

The burning fire was inside the kingfisher's stomach. So the little kingfisher began to writhe in great pain and suffering.

Now the ogress came to collect her find in her fish trap and saw the kingfisher writhing in great pain and suffering. She grabbed a small stick, which was as small as a tall palm tree trunk. She hit the bird and took it home to her family.

She cut open the bird and found the fish.

She cut open the fish and found the wild ox.

She cut open the wild ox and found a log.

She cut open the log and found the seven men carrying their lances and sabers.

She ate the bird.

She ate the fish.

She ate the wild ox. When she was about to finish the ox, she felt quite full.

So she said, "After dinner there is always breakfast. These seven men will be my fine breakfast tomorrow." So she put the seven in a cage.

That night the men knew that they would definitely die if they could not find a way to escape. So they discussed how they could get out of this dire danger and came up with a plan.

"*Hoa maa phaaloo wao,*" ("Let us all speak in tall-tale language,")

"*nee tai hai suang.*" ("to comfort us from this rushing death.")

So they began speaking very loudly, loud enough for the ogress to hear.

The first man said: "Oh, I miss my father."

The second man said: "Yes, me too."

"*Khoi yaak dai naa noi noi,*" ("I wish to have the little bow and arrow,")

"*pho khoi maa ying phi sua nam de.*" ("that belongs to my father, so I could shoot the ogress.")

The third man asked: "*Naa pho cao noi yai paan dai?*" ("How big or small is your father's bow?")

The second man answered: "Oh, it is not that big."

"*Saen khon khuen ma ngoi ka bo kong,*" ("One hundred thousand men could not bend my father's bow,")

"*pho khoi khuen kha sai kong maa.*" ("but my father's left foot could bend it easily.")

The fourth man said:

"*Ying laew khoi yaak dai mo noi noi,*" ("After shooting the ogress, I wish I could have a little cooking pot,")

"*pho khoi maa kaeng de.*" ("that belongs to my father, to cook her.")

The fifth man asked:

"*Mo pho cao noi yai paan dai?*" ("How big or small is your father's little pot?")

The fourth man answered: "Oh, it is not that big."

"*Beuang nueng fod fiang fiang.*" ("One side of the pot is bubbling, making *fiang fiang* sounds.")

"*Beuang nueng fod fai fai.*" ("One side is bubbling, making *fai fai* sounds.")

"*Khon thang lai khii saphao pai khaa.*" (People could board the ship to travel for some merchandise trading.")

"*Dek noi len sabaa nai nawaa.*" ("The little children could play a game of *sabaa* [round vine seeds of about four inches in diameter] in a boat nearby.")

He was implying that the cooking pot was so big that ships could sail on it!

The sixth man said:

"*Kaeng suk laew khoi yaak dai jong noi noi,*" (After the cooking is done, I want a little ladle,")

"*pho khoi maa tak boeng de.*" ("that belongs to my father, to scoop up the ogress soup.")

The seventh man asked:

"*Jong noi noi pho cao nan noi yai paan dai?*" ("How big or small is your father's ladle?")

The sixth man answered:

"*Jong noi noi pho khoi ni,*" ("With my father's little ladle,")

"*tak baad nueng dai baan,*" ("the first scoop, I would get a village,")

"*taan baad nueng dai muang,*" ("the next scoop, I would get a city")

"*tak khiang khiang dai phi huo sua,*" ("the side scoop, I would get the head of the water ogress,") "*jum dai nua phi sua taek nii,*" ("the submerging scoop, I would get the meat of the fleeing ogresses,")

"*phi hong phi haa,*" ("the ghosts who died in distressful accidents and diseases of all kinds,")

"*phi bin bon faa ka taek nii.*" ("and the ghosts flying in the skies who are trying to escape, too.")

The ogress heard the entire conversation and shuddered with nervousness and great fear.

"Oh, no, these men's fathers sound powerfully frightening. If I killed them, their fathers would come after me."

So the ogress opened the cage and let the seven men go.

They went to report their victory to the king, who was willing to give his seven daughters to them.

"Oh, no, we don't want to get married, Your Majesty. We want to go search for the Buddha's noble truth," they told the king.

"But why did you volunteer to fight the wild ox if you don't want to claim the reward?" asked the king.

"We wanted to save the people and the city, so that every one could live in peace," they answered.

"Now that we have done that, we are ready to go to be ordained as Buddhist monks," they explained.

And so they were. And the people of that city continued to prosper and the people were happy.

Note: This story may seem different from most adventure tales, in which the winners claim the rewards. In this case, the seven men could have married the seven daughters and inherited the wealth and ruling power from the king. But the heroes turned down all this to become Buddhist monks. The explanation is that this story is actually a Buddhist riddle story. The seven men represent seven virtues for men. All the obstacles that they have to conquer are their temptations. They have to be able to conquer their own temptations before they are ready to take the Buddha's path to nirvana. Their final temptation is married life with the seven beautiful daughters of the king. They may have set out to fight the wild ox for the rewards, but after going through all kinds of perils, they have realized that those things were uncertain. So their final decision is to search for the highest truth of freeing themselves from all worldly attachments, which include wealth and married life.

THE STINGY BIRD

Retold by Rerai Romyen from a version by Kamphon from Wapipathum School, Mahasarakham, Thailand.

*O*nce an old man went out to work in his rice field, preparing for harvest. He saw a flock of birds swarming in his rice field.

"Oh, those birds are eating my rice grains again. I will catch them," he thought, and he quickly went home to get his net to catch the birds.

Once he was back at his rice field, he cast his net over the flock of birds. "Ha, ha," he laughed triumphantly.

But when he pulled up his net, all but one bird escaped. The old man was dismayed, but thought, "Oh well, one bird. A bird in the net is better than nothing."

He put the bird in his bamboo trap, tied the trap onto his waist, and began walking home, thinking, "A good dinner tonight."

As he was walking, he heard from his trap:

"*Khi thi Khi thi Khi thi*" ("stingy, stingy, stingy")!

The old man looked around to see where the sounds were coming from. "*Khi thi, khi thi, khi thi,*" came the sounds again from the trap.

"What? This bird is calling me a stingy man. I will pluck his feathers and roast him for dinner tonight."

So when he arrived at his house, the man plucked the bird's feathers. "How's that, Bird? You will never call me stingy again."

But as he was roasting the bird over the fire, he heard, "*Khi thi, khi thi, khi thi,*" from the bird.

The old man was angry. "Even when I put it over the fire, this bird is still calling me stingy. After I *eat* it, it won't call me stingy any more!"

The old man put the bird in his mouth and swallowed it whole.

"Aha, now you will never call me stingy again."

But after awhile he heard from his stomach, "*Khi thi, khi thi, khi thi.*"

The old man was furious this time. "Even after I have swallowed you in my stomach, you still called me stingy. I will throw up now."

So he vomited. "Now, you will stop calling me stingy."

But he heard from his vomit, "*Khi thi, khi thi, khi thi.*"

The old man was outraged. "Even after all this, this bird still called me stingy. I will beat it with this huge stick."

So he beat at the vomit with his stick.

"Now you will not call me stingy again."

But the bird flew up from the vomit and landed on the back of his head.

After awhile he heard from his head, "*Khi thi khi thi, khi thi.*"

The old man could control his temper no longer.

"Now I will get rid of this bird once and for all with this stick."

So he waited. When he heard the sounds, "*Khi thi khi thi, khi thi,*" he slammed the huge stick at the sound with all his might.

But he forgot that the bird was on his head. The heavy blow sent the old man to the ground unconscious.

Barely conscious, the old man heard, "*Khi thi, khi thi, khi thi.*" He opened his eyes for the last time and saw the bird flying away in the air.

Yak at Wat Xiang Thong in
Luang Phabang

Nox Kaxum, the baldheaded stork

Lao schoolchildren near Luang Phabang listening to storytellers

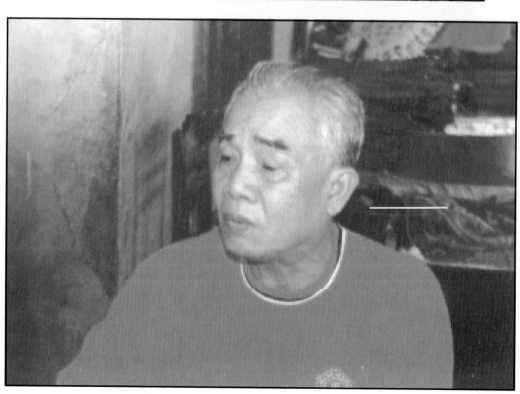

Bounyok Saensounthone, storyteller

Buddhaphisek ceremony in Ban Nong Deun, Suvannakhet, Laos. A new Buddha image is being dedicated. By touching one of the dangling threads, each of the participants can be connected to the sacred spirit of the event.

Wajuppa Tossa showing respect at *Buddhaphisek*

Young girl weaving silk at the Children's Cultural Center in Vientiane

Making *baisii*

Girl with sticky rice basket in hand and fish trap basket over shoulder

Girl at Plain of Jars

Phra Wiangsamai (teller of "Nine Bamboo Clumps")

Spinning silk

Temple at Xiang Thong, Luang Phabang. This mosaic shows the levels of life in the world: animals and people on the earth, Buddha at the top, and his disciples beneath.

Weaving under house

Monks receiving food

**Kongdeuane Nettavong displaying a musical instrument made from a
water buffalo's horn**

PART 9

Tales of Helpful Gods and Spirits

NANG KAIKAEW: THE GIRL AND THE PRECIOUS ROOSTER

Retold by Kongdeuane Nettavong. Translated by Wajuppa Tossa.

*O*nce, long ago, there was a couple who had one daughter. They loved her as their own eyes. They lived happily.

But there came a drastic drought that lasted for years and years. The trees and grass withered and the animals fell dead. People did not have anything to eat or drink. They left their villages to search for forest food such as taros and wild yams to eat instead of rice. Some fell dead while digging up roots. There was no water in any pond, swamp, stream, or river. Even water that came down from the high mountains dried up. The earth became cracked. People followed the dry stream to try to find the source of water.

When the couple saw people going in search of water, they discussed between themselves, "We should go search for water with other villagers. If we are lucky we may be able to have water for our daughter. We may survive."

The couple carried necessary tools and food supplies, carrying their daughter to join the other villagers' procession. After many days of walking, the food supplies were gone. The husband said to his wife, "We need to leave our daughter in the middle of the forest. If we bring her along, we may not have any energy to go on, and we may never find any water for our daughter." The wife agreed.

So they built a little hut and left their daughter there with a raw egg and a lump of sticky rice in her hands. Before leaving, the mother said to her daughter, "My beloved daughter, you must wait for Father and Mother here." With that, they left her there.

The girl waited and waited for her parents, but there was no sign of them. She kept crying and crying. She could not eat rice nor could she drink water. After many days, a chick hatched out of the egg. It became a tiny rooster.

The girl kept feeding the little rooster every single day until it grew big. She taught it to speak a human language. Once it was big enough, it was able to converse with her. She became a little less friendless.

One day the rooster asked her, "My dear girl, why are you so sad and lonely?"

The girl replied, "I miss my parents so much!" Then she recounted the story of how her parents went out in search of water in a faraway land a long time ago. And they had not come back yet.

The rooster felt very sorry for her. In order to repay her kindness in raising him until he was grown, he said to her, "My dear girl, please don't be sad. Tell me what you want. I will help you fulfill your wish."

The girl said, "I would like to have a beautiful city full of people, animals, water, fire, knives, axes, spades and hoes, and everything we need."

Then the rooster told her, "Before dawn, when I crow, you must make a wish for everything that you want."

Before dawn, the rooster crowed, "*Ok lok ok.*" When the girl heard it, she made a wish for everything that she would like to have.

The next day, when she woke up, she saw a beautiful and glorious city with people, animals, water, fire, knives, axes, spades and hoes, and every thing she wished for. The entire city was prosperous, with food and water.

The girl was very delighted to have all that she wished for. But when she looked at the rooster, he looked so sad and lonely. She asked him, "My brother, why are you so sad and lonely?"

The rooster replied, "I have to die because of all the knives that you wished for. Such things are cruel for me. When I die, you must cremate my body!"

Not long after that, the rooster died. So she cremated his body until it was turned to ashes. She buried the ashes near the fence in front of her house. Every day she watered the ashes of the rooster.

Then a gardenia plant grew from the rooster's ashes. The girl continued to take care of the gardenia plant, watering it every day. When the plant was big enough, it bore a single unusually large white flower. It bloomed and permeated the entire city with wonderfully sweet fragrance. After the gardenia flower withered and fell off the plant, she picked it up and put it on the high altar above her bed. Every day she presented flowers, incense, and candles to pay homage to the flower.

Late one night a handsome young man came out of that gardenia flower. The girl was amazed to see this beautiful young man. Every night he would emerge from the gardenia and visit with her. After a while she came to love this magical creature. She realized that it must be her dear rooster finding a way to look after her even after his death. So in time she married the young man. The story doesn't say if the girl's parents were able to return or not. But if they did, they found her well cared for and happily married.

KAMPHA KAI TO: THE ORPHAN AND THE ROOSTER

Retold by Kongdeuane Nettavong. Translated by Wajuppa Tossa.

*O*nce there was an orphan boy who made a living by raising a wild rooster in order to call wild pheasants. His rooster would make its cry and the wild pheasants would come toward it, thinking this was the call of another wild pheasant. Whenever he went to the forest with his rooster, he would get a chicken coop full of pheasants. He saved some for his own food and shared the rest with his neighbors in the village. The villagers called him, Kampha Kai To, or "the Wild Rooster Orphan."

When the boy grew up he married, and his wife thought he should turn his attention to other tasks. One day before he went to bed, his wife consulted with him, "My dear husband, now that it's the rice planting season, you should stop going to get wild pheasants. It's time you built the dikes, prepared the rakes and the ploughs." The orphan agreed with his wife.

The next morning, the orphan got up early. He went under the house, picked up the rooster from the coop, soaked a cloth with warm water, and rubbed the rooster's head, wings, and entire body with love and care. This is the way a good owner cares for his special rooster.

After feeding the rooster, he picked up his lunch bag and walked his buffalo to the field contentedly.

When he got to the little hut in the rice field, the orphan tied the buffalo in the middle of the field and began building dikes, until it was noon. Then he took a rest and had lunch at the hut. After that he pulled out the rakes and the ploughs to fix them. While he was working, he heard the wild pheasants crowing in the forest. He thought about his rooster, "Now he must be crowing and crowing, my dear rooster."

That day, the king of the city came to visit the villagers. He heard that the orphan had many wild pheasants, so he went to visit his house. The orphan's wife greeted the king and brought water for the king as a good hostess.

After resting awhile, the king said to the orphan's wife, "I heard that your husband has a lot of wild pheasants. So I came to visit."

The orphan's wife was intelligent; she understood that the king wanted to have a meal made from the pheasants. So she said, "Today my husband did not go to get wild pheasants and the ones he had, he gave to the neighbors."

The king said to the wife, "Is there any other kind of chicken that tastes like the wild pheasant?" As he was saying that, he noticed the orphan's rooster under the house. So he said, "How about that one?"

The orphan's wife understood that the king would like to eat that rooster. So she prepared it and presented it to the king, not realizing how much the orphan treasured that rooster.

When the orphan returned home, he hurriedly went to see his rooster in the coop under the house. But he found no rooster. So he called to his wife, "My dear wife, where did you put my rooster?"

The wife replied truthfully, "From your rooster, I prepared a meal for the king and he ate it." When the orphan heard that, he was so infuriated that he could not control his temper. He grabbed a stick and chased his wife. She ran away crying. She ran to the king to ask for help.

The king asked her, "What happened to you, woman? Why are you coming to me crying like this?"

She replied, "My husband scolded me and chased me clear out of the house. He was going to beat me up."

The king said, "Why are you quarreling so violently like that?"

"Oh, my husband scolded me because I made you a meal out of his rooster," she replied.

The king said, "Oh, I didn't realize that the orphan loved his rooster that much."

The wife didn't want to admit to the king that she had cooked her husband's prize bird, so she said instead, "Oh, it's not that, your majesty. He scolded me because we had all kinds of meat such as the pigs, the cows, and the buffalo but I only made a meal out of such a little rooster for you. He was angry because the food was not good enough for kings."

When the king heard that, he thought the orphan was a considerate man who honored the king. So he said to the wife, "You may go home and tell your husband that I am promoting him to be *phya*, a lord in my city."

Receiving that order from the king, the wife ran back to her husband with the good news.

When the king reached his palace, he sent his noblemen and ministers to invite the orphan and his wife to have an audience with him. Then the king made a proclamation for the entire city to hear, "From now on, I grant the title of "*phya*" to the orphan. Now every one must call him by this title, "Phya Khampha.""

Since that day, the orphan and his wife have lived happily. This story illustrates the Lao saying, "The husband becomes *phya* because of his dear intelligent wife."

NAMYA WISET: THE MAGIC WATER

Retold by Kongdeuane Nettavong. Translated by Wajuppa Tossa.

*O*nce there was an orphan boy whose parents died when he was very young. The boy begged for rice and food from the villagers daily. The villagers scolded him and cursed him for bothering them. When he was grown he became embarrassed. So he left the village and went to stay in the forest.

The orphan was wandering in the forest aimlessly, eating leaves and grass for food. One day while he was walking in the forest, he saw a bird in a tree. He shot that bird down, and it was a turtle dove. He plucked its feathers and found a sharp stone to cut the bird. When he cut the wattle, he found a lot of rice seeds inside the wattle. So he dried the seeds for planting.

When the rainy season came, the orphan searched for stone from the cliff to make knives. Then he cleared the field and began to plant the rice seeds that he got from the bird's wattle. The orphan took very good care of his rice field, weeding it regularly. After a year, the rice was ripe. Again, he saved the seed and dried it to plant the next year.

After many years of saving and replanting like this, the orphan had many rice fields with good crops of rice. He sold the rice and saved the rest in the granaries. In fact, there was so much rice that he did not have enough granaries to store the seed rice. So he poured some into a hollow tree and some into a hollow stone near his rice fields. There was rice everywhere.

One day the rice birds came and ate the seed rice in the hollow stone. The orphan tried to chase them but failed. So he asked them, "Why are you stealing my seed rice? Don't you know that I worked very hard before I could get it?"

The birds replied, "We are very hungry. That's why we stole your rice. Please forgive us." The orphan thought about how he had felt when he begged for rice from others and they scolded him. The birds were just like him. So he felt sympathetic toward the birds and let them eat his rice.

After the rice birds finished eating, the leader of the birds said to the orphan, "We thank you very much for sharing your rice with us. We have nothing to repay your kindness but this little ball of gold. Please put it with the seed rice left in the hollow stone." With that instruction, the birds flew away.

The orphan took the gold and put it with the rice in the hollow stone, as he was told. The next morning he went to see his seed rice in the hollow stone. Everything in the hold had turned to water. He felt bad about losing his seed rice, but when he looked at the water carefully, it was crystal clear as a mirror. So he scooped up a handful of the water to drink.

After the water fell into his stomach, the orphan felt something strange happening to his body. His complexion became newer and brighter. He felt much stronger. When he looked at his own reflection in the water, he found that he was more handsome than before.

One day a hunter went hunting in the forest. He shot a deer and carried it on his shoulder. As he approached the orphan's rice fields, he found the water in the hollow stone. He put down the dead deer and drank that water. After the water went down into his stomach, he felt that his body was stronger. He splashed some water on the dead deer. And lo and behold, the deer got up and ran away.

The hunter ran after the deer, but he could not catch up with it. While he was following his deer, he saw the orphan. So he asked the orphan, "That water belongs to you?" The orphan said, "Yes, it does. It's magical water. It can bring the dead to life. It can make the old young again. And the plain and ugly can become attractive and beautiful."

The hunter wished to have the water. So he poured some into his bamboo pipe, but the water would not be contained. It kept leaking out no matter how many times he tried. So he hurriedly went home.

After getting home, he went to report to the king, "Your Majesty, there is magic water that belongs to the orphan in the faraway place! The water could cure the sick and make them well again!"

When the king heard about this, he sent his noblemen and ministers to bring the orphan to cure his daughter, who had been sick in bed for many years.

The orphan put three drops of the magic water in the princess's mouth. Suddenly she got up and began talking as if she had never been ill before. Her complexion seemed to be renewed and bright. She became healthy and perfectly plump. After the princess recovered, the king gave his daughter to the orphan to be his wife. He also offered bountiful silver and gold, but the orphan would not take them. All he wanted was a knife and an axe. Then he took leave of the king and returned to live in the forest as before.

The orphan returned with his knife and axe and began again to clear away the land to make rice fields and plant abundant rice seeds. His rice fields yielded good crops, and he gave away his rice to the poor and the needy. He lived happily but simply and enjoyed giving rice away to the people who needed it, just as he had once needed rice.

People praised the orphan for his kindness and his good heart. They say that after his death he turned into a tall and long range of mountains, called "*phuu hai.*"

And after that, people named their rice containers "*hai khao*" and their water containers "*hai nam*" to guarantee that they would never lack rice and water ever again.

YHAA NUAT MAEW: THE MAGIC PLANT

Retold by Kongdeuane Nettavong. Translated by Wajuppa Tossa.

A long time ago when the earth was first created, Indra was the highest god who overlooked everything on earth, including all animals and humans.

All creatures on earth lived together peacefully. Nobody had power over anybody else. The small creatures looked up to the larger creatures as their helpers. The large creatures never mistreated the little ones. All lived in honesty and contentment.

Traveling in those days was convenient. The creatures need only make a wish and they would be at the place they wanted to go in a moment.

Indra resided in heaven, while his *thewada* (the celestial beings) would travel the earth to look after all earthlings.

Unlike on earth, there were no animals in heaven, except for one. Indra allowed one cat in heaven. This one cat was given all kinds of privileges; even the other *thewada* had to treat the cat with respect. The cat realized this fact and became very arrogant, since he knew that he was Indra's favorite.

Every Buddhist holy day, on the fifteenth nights of the full moon and of the waning moon, Indra would bathe in the holy water. The *thewada* took turns bringing the holy water from the Himmaphan Forest for Indra to bathe in. Then Indra's bath water would be sent to earth to water the plants. The *thewada* would recite words of incantation and blow the sacred water down to earth, and it would become rain in different places on earth.

The holy day arrived again for Indra to bathe. One of the *thewada* soared down to the sacred pond and brought the water up to Indra's hall. The *thewada* carefully prepared the golden bath tub filled with the holy water brought from the Himmaphan Forest. When everything was done, he turned around to leave the bathing room for Indra. Indra's cat, who was lying around that area, opened his little eye and saw that the *thewada* was leaving. He quickly jumped into that bath tub with a big *splash* that made the *thewada* turn around to see what happened.

The *thewada* was so infuriated that a great big whip appeared in his hand. He ran to the bath tub and brought down the whip on the cat countless times. The water splashed all over the bathing room and the cat's screams sounded throughout the entire heavens. The *thewada* was so angered that he whipped the cat again and again.

The cat, which had never been touched or hurt by anyone, became so frightened that he ran and jumped all over the place until he fell down to earth. He fell down right into the flower garden of a widow. He was so scared that he ran around trying to hide in flower bushes. The cat writhed and squirmed in the bushes until the flowers were all smashed and trampled.

The *thewada* was punished, and Indra made a proclamation that from then on whoever hurt that cat would be most sinful and would have bad *karma*.

As for the widow, she was so angry about the flowers that she went to get a whip to beat the cat. But because the cat was hiding in a thick bush, she could not see it. She was waiting for the cat to come out, but the cat never came out. The widow waited until she had an urge to pee, but she was determined to keep an eye on the cat. She refused to leave and go to the toilet.

The cat became so hungry that he took a mouthful of the flowers and ate them. Soon after the flowers reached the cat's stomach, he felt his pains disappear. He fell right asleep in the bush.

The widow waited and waited. By the time she finally gave up and ran to the bathroom, she was in pain. So she called her granddaughter, "Granddaughter, go and get a medicinal flower from the garden for me."

The girl ran to the garden, but she had never seen the medicinal flower before. She looked and she looked but she could not find one flower that would be medicinal. She was pushing and pulling the plants around where the cat was. The cat was so frightened that he cried loudly. The girl was also frightened of the cat's cry. She stood there and stared into the bush. She saw Indra's cat's whiskers right in front of her eyes. She pulled a few flowers that looked like the cat's whiskers and took them to her grandmother.

The widow took a handful of flowers and chewed them in her mouth. After swallowing the chewed flowers, the widow's pain was gone. When she heard of how the girl found the medicinal flowers, she went to pick up the cat. She felt very thankful to the cat as it had helped her granddaughter find the medicinal flowers. The cat became her favorite animal after that. Nobody was allowed to hurt that cat.

From then on, whenever anyone has pains from bladder problems, it is recommended that a handful of the plant be boiled to drink as tea. To honor the cat for pointing out this secret, the plant was named after the cat. Since then the plant with medicinal flowers is called, "*yhaa nuat maew*" or "cat's whiskers grass."

PART 10

Place Legends

The term *legend* has two meanings for the Lao people: *phuen sueb,* which means historical chronicles or accounts; and *nithan a-thi bay hed,* which means explanatory tales. Legends have an important place in Lao culture, as they are regarded as true historical accounts as well as true accounts that can be used to explain how things happen the way they do. This chapter includes historical chronicles that are well known to Lao people as well as tales explaining natural phenomena.

THE STORY OF VIENTIANE

Retold by Wajuppa Tossa.

In the old time there were three kingdoms in Laos, one in the north called Muang Sua, present-day Luang Phabang; one in the central area, Phainaam, present-day Vientiane; and one in the south, Champasak. This story tells how Phya Fa-ngum, king of the northern kingdom, took control of the central kingdom. (Phya is a title equivalent to king.)

*O*nce there was a peculiar city surrounded by thorny bamboo clumps, which created the city walls, protecting it from any enemy. The city was called Phainaam (*phai* means bamboo; *naam* means thorns).

At that time there was a city ruler named Phya Fa-ngum. He was the most powerful king during that time. He had led his army to subdue many cities. Once, after one of his battles, he led his army to Phainaam, intending to seize the city. However, there was no way for his army to enter the city. He thought of many ways to conquer the city, but nothing seemed to work. For more than ten days he tried to overthrow the city, but he could not. He considered burning the city down, but felt sorry for the women, children, and elderly folks. These people took no part in the war, but they had to suffer its consequences.

Phya Fa-ngum then came up with a brilliant plan. He ordered his soldiers to wrap their bullets and arrowheads with gold sheet. Then he ordered them to shoot those bullets and arrows at the bamboo clumps around the city. After that was done, he led his army away from the city, leaving a spy behind.

The people of Phainaam, seeing that Phya Fa-ngum's army retreated, came out to conduct their lives in their usual ways. It happened that some of the people saw the arrowheads and bullets covered with gold. These people then spread a rumor that there were gold arrows and bullets stuck to every bamboo clump around the city. Upon hearing the rumor, both the common subjects and the rulers of the city took no time to reason or to think of the consequences. They all went to cut down every bamboo bush, searching for gold. Finally, the city had no walls for protection.

Once all the city walls were cleared away, Phya Fa-ngum's spy sent a message to Phya Fa-ngum, informing him of the news. Phya Fa-gnum then led his army to take over Phainaam easily. After that the city was no longer called Phainaam. This is the present-day city of Viengkhan (Vientiane).

THE CASTING OF PHA BANG

Retold by Kongdeuane Nettavong. Translated by Wajuppa Tossa.

*L*ong, long ago there was a revered saintly monk, Chunlanaga, who was endowed with magical power. Chunlanaga wished to make Buddhism a long-lasting religion, one that would endure for 5,000 years or more. So the monk went all over Sri Lanka (Ceylon) to persuade people to contribute to a ceremony of casting a Buddha image. The ceremony was to be held under the patronage of the king of Sri Lanka, Lord Indra, and other celestial beings, Brahmans, and ascetics.

Once agreement was reached, Chunlanaga started collecting from the people. He collected silver, gold, copper, and brass wares, which could be melted down. He had people bring flowers, incense, and candles for the ceremony. When the appointed time came, the patrons of the ceremony took all the collected metal objects and dropped them into a melting pot. After the process was finished, the newly cast Buddha image was named Pha Bang*. The celebration was held and lasted for seven days. The *"Buddhaphisek"* ceremony,** conducted by a number of senior monks, was held on the night of the full moon.

Because of the auspicious day of the *Buddhaphisek* ceremony, the Pha Bang was endowed with great magical power. It was so powerful that all creatures on earth and in the heavens must worship Pha Bang. The saintly and revered monk, Chunlanaga, brought with him five valuable and magic crystals from the shrine where the ashes of Buddha were kept. He planned to put those five objects in the body of Pha Bang. But while the chanting and praying of the Buddhist monks was going on, the first crystal went flying toward the Pha Bang and sank itself into the Buddha image's forehead; the second one rested in the Buddha image's chin; the third one in the right hand; the fourth one in the left hand; and the last one right in the center of the image's chest. So that concluded the casting of Pha Bang, but the fame and reputation of sacredness of the Buddha image spread out all over the land.

Many centuries later, the king of Inthapattha City, Cambodia, went to Sri Lanka to ask for the Pha Bang image to be brought to his city. Many generations went by, and then the Pha Bang was removed from Viengkham City*** to Muang Sua, now the city of Luang Pha Bang, the old Royal Capital of Laos, by King Suyachakkapatti Phenepheo, the king of Muang Sua.

The image now is at the old palace, which has been made into the national museum of Laos in Luang Phabang. And the name of the city was changed to use the same name as this Buddha image. It is one of the most important images, as it is believed to have magical power that will protect people from harm.

----

*In Lao, *pha* is a pronoun referring to a Buddhist monk or a Buddha image, and *bang* means "thin" or "little."

** The religious ritual held during the casting of Buddha images.

*** Present-day Vientiane.

THE LEGEND OF PHU SI

Retold by Chanpheng Singphet, Children's Culture Center, Luang Phabang. Collected and retold in English by Wajuppa Tossa.

This is the story of a mountain that stands right in front of the royal palace in Luang Phabang. In this tale Queen Sita of the Ramayana epic lives in the palace. In the Ramayana, the Monkey King, Hanuman, is a friend to her husband, Rama, and a rescuer of Queen Sita.

*O*nce Queen Sida wanted to have tiger ear mushrooms for her meal. But in the northern Lao language this mushroom is called monkey ear mushrooms. Queen Sida asked the Monkey King, Hanuman, to go search for the mushrooms for her from the mountain in Oudomxay (another province in northern Laos, situated to the northwest of Luang Phabang).

"Could you please go and get the mushrooms from Oudomxay Mountain for me?" said Sida.

"Yes, my Lady," answered Hanuman.

So Hanuman flew to Oudomxay Mountain and gathered some mushrooms for Queen Sida. He returned with a basket full of mushrooms for her. But Queen Sida looked at them and said,

"Oh, no, this is not the kind of mushroom I would like to have. Please go and bring some others." She did not want to say that she really wanted "monkey ear" mushrooms, for she thought that it would offend Hanuman, who is, after all, a monkey.

"Yes, my Lady," said Hanuman.

He soared in the sky to pick up more mushrooms at Oudomxay Mountain. After awhile he returned with another basket full of mushrooms for Queen Sida. She again examined the mushrooms.

"Oh, no, this is still not the kind of mushroom I would like to have. Please go bring some other kinds."

"Yes, my Lady," said Hanuman.

He soared in the sky to pick up more mushrooms at Oudomxay Mountain. After awhile he returned with another basket full of mushrooms for Queen Sida. She again examined the mushrooms.

"Oh, no, this is still not the kind of mushroom I would like to have. How can I tell you what kind of mushroom I would like?"

Hanuman was puzzled. He did not know exactly what kind of mushroom he should get for Queen Sida. Queen Sida herself could have told Hanuman what kind of mushrooms she would like if they were not monkey ear mushrooms. Then Hanuman had an idea. "Don't worry, your majesty. I will bring what you want."

Hanuman flew off, and soon he was back again. With a great PLOP . . . he deposited the entire top of Oudomxay Mountain right in front of the palace!

"There you are, Your Majesty! What you want MUST be here somewhere. Just pick whatever you like!"

Ever after that a great mountain has stood right at the door of the royal palace in Luang Phabang. The mountain is called "Phu Sida" for Queen Sida. But sometimes it is just called "Phu Si" for short. It is also said that the top of Oudomxay Mountain is missing . . . it is flat on the top, for the top is in Luang Phabang.

PHYA SIKHOTTABONG

From *Sikhhottabong* by Duangkhai Luangphasi. Retold by Wajuppa Tossa.

*O*nce, long ago, in the central part of Laos, there was a poor couple who had a son named Thao Sii. Thao Sii was quite clever, but mischievous. So his parents decided to have Thao Sii ordained as a novice monk. After being a novice for eight years, he asked for permission to leave the monastery. When he became a layman, his title was changed to Xiang. Xiang Sii realized that his parents were growing old, so he wanted to take care of them in return.

His parents were concerned about Xiang Sii's future. So they decided to take Xiang Sii to the city ruler. They wanted Xiang Sii to be the king's servant and to do whatever the king wished him to do.

The king ordered Xiang Sii and other men to go to the forest to collect resin from dipterocarpous trees. Because Xiang Sii looked thin and weak, his friends asked him to cook for them instead of collecting resin. One day while the sticky rice was being steamed, Xiang Sii went to cut a branch of a black kapok tree to make a *mai kadaam* —a spatula for stirring the sticky rice after it is steamed.

When the rice was cooked, he poured it onto a pannier basket and began to stir the rice to cool it off a little before putting it in the bamboo box. But he became much alarmed because the sticky rice turned black when the spatula touched it. Xiang Sii was actually frightened that the rice turned black, because it could be a bad omen. It is believed that when one cooks white rice, it is not supposed to change color. If it does change, to red, yellow, black, or any other color besides white, it means there is going to be a disaster.

Being afraid that his friends would find out about it, Xiang Sii immediately ate the entire pannier of black rice. After he finished that black rice, a miracle took place. Xiang Sii's body changed. He became a big strong man! He might have been as strong as many elephants. To test his own new strength, Xiang Sii reached up to pull down a great big dipterocarpous tree. To all his friends' awe and amazement, the tree was bent down.

Now in the city of Vientiane, there were many elephants invading the city, destroying houses, and hurting people. The people, faced with dire danger, were running for their lives. The king of Vientiane called for an assembly of noblemen and ministers for consultation.

He ordered them to go search for a brave person to conquer the elephants. The king promised to give a reward to the conqueror: "Whoever can conquer the elephants, I shall give him my daughter's hand in marriage."

Upon hearing the announcement, Xiang Sii hurried to the forest to cut a black kapok tree to make a giant *tabong* club and headed for Vientiane. Once there, he bravely brandished his giant club, chasing the elephants out of the city. All elephants but one ran away from the city. Xiang Sii fought with the leader of the elephants for three days and three nights before it gave in.

After conquering the elephants, the king called Xiang Sii to claim his reward. He arranged a wedding between his daughter, Nang Kheowkhom, and Xiang Sii, as promised. The king also sent Xiang Sii and his wife to rule a city called Muang Sikhot. Since then the city of Muang Sikhot has been called "Muang Sikhottabong." The new king, Xiang Sii, was now called "Phya Sikhottabong."

Later a jealous minister went to talk to the king in private, saying that, with his miraculous power, Phya Sikhottabong might one day overthrow the king of Vientiane. The gullible Vientiane king easily believed such slander. Therefore he told his daughter to find out what made Phya Sikhottabong have extraordinary strength and how he could be conquered.

Nang Kheowkhom pretended to be so sweet and loving that Phya Sikhottabong was deceived. He told her all his secrets because of his love for her. One of those secrets was to reveal the only way he could be killed, by spearing him at a certain point on his body. Once the king of Vientiane found out the secret, he invited Phya Sikhottabong to visit him in Vientiane. And there he had him murdered.

After Phya Sikhottabong was killed, his body was floated down the river on a raft. When the people of Muang Sikhottabong caught sight of their dead king, they became very frightened. The people mourned and cried for their king for seven days and seven nights, recalling the king's great deeds. They also recalled that Phya Sikhottabong had ruled the city justly and peaceably.

And so the story of this hero, Xiang Sii, who became Phya Sikhottabong, is told and retold in the city of Muang Sikkhotabong in the Khammuan region of Laos to this very day.

THE PLAIN OF JARS:
THONG HAI HIN

Retold by Wajuppa Tossa.

On the high plain around Phounsavang, Xiangkhoung, in northern Laos, there is an area covered with large stone jars. No one knows their origin, but various stories are told. Here is one very short one. See also a longer version of this story in Part 12.

*O*nce there was a kingdom ruled by a cruel king named Thao Angka. The people could not tolerate the king, so they asked Thao Juang to help. Thao Juang marched his soldiers down to defeat Thao Angka. Once his army had won, he ordered huge jars made to make rice wine to keep his army happy. They then celebrated their victory by drinking wine from the jars.

THE FOREST GIBBONS OF LAOS: NANG ZANEE KHUAN

Retold by Kongdeuane Nettavong. Translated by Wajuppa Tossa.

*O*nce, long ago, there was a childless married couple. They wished to have a child of their own. So they went to ask for a baby from a *thewada* or celestial being, who resided in a tall tree near a pond.

"So, you want to have a baby of your own!" boomed a voice from the tree.

"Yes, we would like to have a baby. Please give us a baby," said the couple.

"You may have a baby. Go home now and you will hear a cry like a gibbon's cry. That will be your baby," commanded the *thewada*.

The married couple returned home as they were told. As they were approaching their home, they heard a cry that sounded like a baby's or maybe a gibbon. When they got closer they saw a baby gibbon lying on its side.

"Oh, my baby," said the couple. "We thank the *thewada* for our baby," they said gratefully.

They raised the baby with love and care. However, the baby always cried, "*kuk, kuk, kuiy, kuiy,*" all the time. It did sound just like a gibbon. The baby's cry sounded in heaven day and night. The god Indra could no longer stand the cry. So he called for a volunteer to go down to earth to see who was crying.

Once the volunteer came down, he found that the cry came from the couple's house. The baby had been crying for her gibbon mother. So he tried to help the baby get back to its gibbon mother. He approached the baby with a banana. When the baby saw the banana, it ran after Indra's volunteer and grabbed the banana. The human mother ran after the baby to try to catch it, but she was too slow. The baby jumped up and down while running away into the forest. The human mother followed the baby into the forest. After days, weeks, months, and years had passed, the baby gibbon regained his gibbon nature, swinging from tree to tree. Finally the mother gibbon found the baby gibbon and hugged it. The mother gibbon swung from tree to tree with the baby gibbon hanging on to her breast. The mother gibbon would not allow the baby to hold on to her back, for fear that the human mother would take the baby away.

Meanwhile, the human mother kept following the baby, but she could not catch up with her baby as she could not climb trees. All she could do was cry,

"Kuiy pong, kuiy pong." ("Listen to my gibbon call for you.") *"Kuiy pong, kuiy pong."*

"Khanong mae pen khon." ("My heels are growing hair.")

"Bo pen khon, bo pen khon khue look laew" ("I am no longer a human, just like you.")

"Kuiy pong kuiy pong." ("Listen to my gibbon call for you.") *"Kuiy pong, kuiy pong."*

She kept on crying for her baby, but it never returned to her. If you go into the deep forest, you may hear the cry. Then you will know that the human mother is still running after her baby, crying,

"Kuiy pong, kuiy pong." ("Listen to my gibbon call for you.") *"Kuiy pong, kuiy pong."*

" Khanong mae pen khon." ("My heels are growing hair.")

"Bo pen khon, bo pen khon khue look laew." ("I am no longer a human, just like you.")

"Kuiy pong kuiy pong." ("Listen to my gibbon call for you.") *"Kuiy pong, kuiy pong."*

PHU PHA PHU NANG: PRINCE MOUNTAIN AND PRINCESS MOUNTAIN

Retold by Kongdeuane Nettavong. Translated by Wajuppa Tossa.

On the right bank of the Mekong River near Siangman Village, opposite Luang Phabang, there are two mountains, called "Phu Pha" or Prince Mountain, and "Phu Nang" or Princess Mountain. These two mountains look like two human beings lying on their backs. The story about these two mountains has been passed down from one generation to the next, right down to the present day.

*O*nce upon a time there was a very poor woodcutter who had a wife and twelve daughters. Because they were so poor the couple took their children to the forest one day and abandoned them there. The girls wandered around the forest, and soon they met an ogress, who had a daughter called Kanghi. The ogress took the girls to her home and raised them with her own daughter.

They stayed with the ogress until they were grown up. One day, the girls decided to escape. The ogress went out searching for them. When she was about to catch them, they hid in the mouth of the King of Bulls. The ogress gave up the search and returned home. The twelve girls continued their journey. When they arrived at a city, the king saw them and fell in love with them. He married all of them.

When the ogress found out that the girls had married the king, she was very angry, so she set out for her revenge. She transformed herself into a beautiful girl and went to see the king. The king fell in love with her and made her his queen.

Not long after that she pretended to be ill. She would not eat anything, so she grew pale and thin. She asked the king to consult an astrologer to find out about her illness. Then she transformed herself into an astrologer, waiting for the king's men to come to consult her. She said that the twelve sisters were the cause of her illness. The king must have the eyes of the twelve sisters taken out for a sacrifice and send them away. Otherwise, she would die.

The king agreed. After getting the eyes of the twelve sisters, the ogress sent them to her daughter, Kanghi, to keep.

At that time, the king's twelve wives were pregnant. The angry king still believed his cruel wife, so he had them locked up in a cave with no food. Only the son of the youngest sister was born living, but she kept the child hidden away.

Later, a wild rooster came to live with them and gave them some rice to eat, so the wives survived. When the son of the twelfth sister grew up, she revealed to her sisters that her child was alive. One day the young man left his mother and aunts and took the wild rooster into the nearby village. There he placed the rooster in cockfights and was able to win. At sunset, the village children gave him food, which he brought to his mother and aunts.

Shortly after that the young man went to take part in some games in the king's palace. He was a very good player, so the king asked to see him. When the king asked him about his family, the young man said he was the son of the youngest of the twelve sisters. The king knew then that this was his own son. So he took the young man to live in the palace, giving him the name "Phouthasen." Every day he would sneak out food to give to his mother and aunts.

When the ogress found out who the boy really was, she decided to kill him. She pretended to be ill again. One day she said to the king: "The only medicine that can cure me is in my own city, and the only person who can go and fetch the medicine for me is Phouthasen." So the king sent him to get the medicine, as the queen wished. Phouthasen asked for a good magic flying horse for the journey. Before he set out, the ogress gave him a letter and said to him: "Take this letter to my daughter, Kanghi, and she will give you many things."

Phouthasen tied the letter to his horse's neck and set out on his journey. After a while he grew tired, so he stopped for a rest near a hermit's hut. After he and his horse fell fast asleep, the ascetic came over and saw the letter. He read the message. "Kanghi, my daughter, when this young man comes to you, please capture him and kill him at once. He is our enemy."

The hermit felt sorry for the young man so he rewrote the letter: "This young man is our king's son, and he is to become your husband. Please welcome him as such."

When the young man came to Kanghi, she opened the letter and read it. She was very pleased and was delighted to make him her husband because he was very handsome. And for his part, Phouthasen fell deeply in love with Kanghi as well . . . even though she was the daughter of an ogress.

Later, when they were at the palace, Kanghi showed him around the grounds, pointing out many wondrous things like the magic lemons, the palace where the twelve ladies' eyes were kept, and where her mother's heart was kept too. Phouthasen was very pleased to see all of these things, and started looking for a way to escape and to bring back the eyes to his mother and his aunts.

One day he asked Kanghi to arrange a big banquet and to invite all of her followers to come and enjoy it. He himself gave his wife and her men a lot of drink, and soon they got drunk and fell asleep. When they were all sleeping soundly, he went to collect the eyes, the ogress's heart, the magic lemons, and other magic things. Then he got on his horse and rode away into the night. When Kanghi and her men awoke and saw that her husband was missing, they set out in search of him. Phouthasen had expected that, so he started to throw some of the magic things in their path. He threw down a magic potion and it created a barrier of thorny bamboo forest.

Eventually Kanghi and her men made their way through it and continued to follow Phouthasen. Then he threw down another magic potion, and this one brought about a turbulent river full of huge waves. It was impossible for Kanghi to cross the river. She cried out to him, begging him to come back to her. But he would not come back, and after awhile Kanghi gave up and led her men back home. She was so broken-hearted at losing Phouthasen that she became very ill and could neither eat nor sleep. In a very short time she died. But before she died, she put a curse on Phouthasen , saying :

"May you die for love, just as I have done."

Meanwhile, Phouthasen returned to his home. He gave the eyes back to his mother and his aunts. Then he squeezed the juice of the magic lemons into their eyes, and everyone's sight was restored. His mother and aunts were, of course, delighted to be able to see again.

Then Phouthasen set off to his father's palace. The wicked ogress saw him and became angry and amazed, because she had given Kanghi orders to kill him. How could he have come back again? She became so furious that she forgot to maintain her identity as a beautiful young princess. She was transformed into an ogress once more. She charged at Phouthasen in her rage, hoping to kill him, but Phouthasen pierced her heart with his sword and she dropped down dead immediately. After that, Phouthasen went to bring his mother and his aunts to live in the palace again. Then he said goodbye to his mother, his father, and his aunts, and went back to the home of his wife, Kanghi. He still loved her, though he had had to finish off the wicked ogress and restore his mother and aunts to the palace before he could return to her.

To his sorrow, Phouthasen found on his arrival that his wife, Kanghi, had already died. He suddenly felt so overwhelmed by his love for her that he could no longer stand. He collapsed and died with his head on her feet.

Now the *thewada* in the heavens thought this was not as it should be, because in the future women, learning from Kanghi's story, would not trust men at all. Therefore the *thewada* came down and changed the position of Phouthasen's body so that Kanghi's head would be at Phouthasen's feet and he would be lying on his back. Lao people believe that men are leaders, so their heads must be in a higher position than women's.

The ancient people of Laos told this story, and it has been handed down from generation to generation. It is said that the bodies of Kanghi and Phouthasen became Phu Pha Phu Nang, Prince Mountain and Princess Mountain. These mountains can still be seen to this very day. They are just like two human beings lying on their backs.

PART 11

Origin Myths of the Lao People

Lao history was not known to scholars outside of Laos until the fourteenth century, when King Fa Ngum, with Khmer backing, succeeded in uniting Laos and much of present-day northeastern Thailand into Lan Xang, the kingdom of a million elephants.

Yet the Lao people themselves have known their history since the beginning of time. They tell of the origin of their people in the myth "The Great Gourd from Heaven." This myth not only tells where the Lao people came from, but also tells about Lao cosmology, which consists of the world of Thaen, the world of human beings, and the world of celestial beings, the *devata* (*thewada*). Thaen is the great god in heaven who is the creator of all the earth and its inhabitants. Thaen also sent down Khoun Bulom, the first king of the humans. The story of Khoun Bulom himself is part of an origin myth of the Lao people. To the Lao it is also a historical chronicle. Almost all Lao people know the name of Lord Bulom and consider him their hero.

THE GREAT GOURD FROM HEAVEN: ALL HUMANITY FROM THE SAME PLACE

Retold by Wajuppa Tossa.

This myth tells how the first King, Khoun Bulom (Lord Bulom) was born to earth; how the earth was troubled because of the gigantic gourd; how Khoun Bulom requested help from heaven; and how the earth was populated with humans, animals, plants, jewels, and other things.

*L*ong, long ago the earth was covered with dense forest, and one enormous creeper grew out of the forest and stretched right up to the sky. It had only one gourd hanging from it, and this gourd was very, very big. The gods in heaven had a meeting and decided that the earth should be inhabited, so one of the gods was sent down with his followers. His name was Khoun Bulom, and he had two wives, Yommala and Akkai.

There were no men or animals on earth at this time, just gods and some spirits. The earth was very dark because of the huge gourd that blocked out the light from the sun. Khoun Bulom sent a messenger to the Great God of heaven asking for help. The Great God, Phya In, ordered some gods to come down to the earth to cut away the creeper and to make holes in the gourd, too.

As soon as they cut away the huge creeper, sunlight shone all over the earth, and it became a very bright, very pleasant place indeed. But making holes in the gourd was a difficult task. At first the gods used a pointed iron bar heated in the fire. As soon as they made the hole in the gourd, many human beings started to crawl out from the center of the gourd.

Because these people had to push their way out through the tiny, dark, sooty hole that the iron bar had burnt in the side of the gourd, they had dark complexions. The hole was quite small, and the human beings found it difficult to squeeze through. The gods saw this, so they made another hole, this time with an axe. This axe made a big clean hole in the side of the gourd, and it was not difficult for the humans to get out. The second batch of humans had lighter complexions than those who came out first because the hole was not burnt.

But all humans came from the same place. Those who came first were the big brothers and sisters, and those who came later were the younger brothers and sisters. They were very closely related. The colors of their skin were not a problem for them at all. These first human beings are the ancestors of all humanity. From that place they spread out all over the world. They adapted themselves to the various climates and natural environments in different places. But the important thing is that they came out from the same place and were the same human beings, and they truly loved one another as brothers and sisters.

When all human beings had come out, the gods pierced yet another hole in the gourd and many animals came out—elephants, horses, cows and so on—and after them many things came out for the human beings to use to make life beautiful. Jewels of all kinds, and gold and silver.

The Lao people have handed this story down from generation to generation, and it shows how every tribe is as worthy of honor and as significant as all the others, because they are all brothers and sisters who come from the same place.

KHOUN BULOM

Retold in English by Wajuppa Tossa.

This story of Khoun Bulom begins with the opening of the giant gourd and continues with Khoun Bulom's adventures. This account includes a slightly different version of the "Great Gourd of Heaven" story told above.

The story of Khoun Bulom takes place in two worlds: one the world of Thaen, the highest celestial being in heaven, and the other the human sphere on earth. In those days the celestial beings and the humans could travel back and forth to visit one another.

There were once three human leaders, named Pu Lang Xoeng, Khoun Khan, and Khoun Khet. They built their territories on earth, Muang Lum, the lower world. They made a living by hunting, fishing, and planting rice. Thus, the people enjoyed eating meat, fish, and rice. Thaen sent his messenger down from heaven to tell the three lords to follow his instructions, in the following verse:

Kin khao hai bok nai.	Eating rice, you might let your Lord know.
Kin ngai hai bok kae Thaen.	Eating late morning meal, you must tell Thaen also.
Kin sin ko hai song kha.	Eating (an animal's) meat, you must send its legs.
Kin pa ko hai song hoi hai Thaen.	Eating fish, you must send some to Thaen.

The people neglected Thaen's command. So he sent his messenger for the second time:

Kin khao hai bok nai.	Eating rice, you might let your Lord know.
Kin ngai hai bok kae Thaen.	Eating late morning meal, you must tell Thaen also.
Kin sin ko hai song kha.	Eating (an animal's) meat, you must send its legs.
Kin pa ko hai song hoi hai Thaen.	Eating fish, you must send some to Thaen.

The people still neglected Thaen's instruction. So Thaen tried one more time to instruct them in how they should behave:

Kin khao hai bok nai.	Eating rice, you might let your Lord know.
Kin ngai hai bok kae Thaen.	Eating late morning meal, you must tell Thaen also.

| *Kin sin ko hai song kha.* | Eating (an animal's) meat, you must send its legs. |
| *Kin pa ko hai song hoi hai Thaen.* | Eating fish, you must send some to Thaen. |

The people still failed to do what Thaen had asked of them. After this third attempt to teach them how to behave, Thaen became so insulted that he sent a flood to Muang Lum, and the great flood injured and killed many people. The three leaders realized that they were the cause of Thaen's wrath, so they built a raft, put their wives and children on the raft, and went to heaven to visit Thaen. Thaen spoke the following verse:

Su bo yi ci bo thao.	If you had no respect, you would never reach old age.
Su bo yam cao ci bo yuen.	If you had no fear, you would not live long.
Su bo fang khwam a-yu su bo mi	If you did not obey me, your age would never reach
thoeng song hoi khuab.	two hundred.

At last the humans understood how to behave. After the flood was over, the three human lords went to pay respect to Thaen and asked for permission to go down to earth again. Thaen gave them a buffalo with beautiful horns and sent them to Na Noi Oy Nu (Muang Thaeng, now Dien Bien Phu in Vietnam.) After three years the buffalo died, and from its nostrils sprouted a vine with three giant gourds. Pu Lang Xoeng heard noises inside the gourds, so he pierced a hole in one with a glowing red fired drill. From the hole came many people. Khoun Khan used a huge chisel to pierce another hole. From that hole came more people; it took three more days for all the people to come out. The people from the first hole split into two groups: one was called Tai Lom and the other Tai Lee. Those from the second hole split into three groups: Tai Lo, Tai Loeng, and Tai Kwang.

At first the people did not know how to survive. Pu Lang Xoeng taught them how to survive and instructed them to become husbands and wives and build households. He taught them to respect their elders and to have funeral ceremonies. The Tai Lom and Tai Lee were instructed to have cremation for the deceased, but the other groups were told to have burial ceremonies. A flag must be placed at the grave and a small hut built so the living could send rice and water to the spirits of the deceased. Those who could not build a hut must prepare a place in their own home for this purpose. They must call the spirit of the deceased to come and have food.

The people in those days could live until they were 300 years old. More and more people populated the earth. They were too many for Pu Lang Xoeng, Khoun Lang, and Khoun Khet to manage. So they went to Thaen and asked for help. Thaen sent his helpers, Khoun Kha and Khoun Khong, down, but they could do nothing much, because they were intoxicated most of the time. The three original human leaders decided to go ask Thaen for help again. Thaen called back Khoun Kha and Khoun Khong and sent Khoun Bulom, who came down with many bards and wise people. Yet there were still troubles. So Khoun Bulom sent his messenger to ask for help from Thaen. This time Thaen sent a messenger to teach people how to plant vegetables and fruit. The people were also taught how to weave and make tools. The messenger also taught people what to do and what not to do. Once Thaen was certain that the people could take care of themselves, he told them not to travel back and forth to heaven again. He had the bridge to heaven collapsed.

After awhile the vine of the gourds became overgrown and blocked the sunlight. Khoun Bulom ordered many people to cut down the vine, but nobody could do it. At last, he sent an old couple, Pu Nyoe and Ya Nyoe, to cut down the vine. The old couple sacrificed their lives to do so. Before they undertook the task, they asked people to remember them by calling their names to join every activity. Thus, the word "*nyoe*" appears after Lao action words (verbs). When people are going to eat, they say, "*Kin yoe*" ("Please eat, Grandma and Grandpa Nyoe").

After the giant vine was cut, the human world prospered again. Later, Khoun Bulom had seven sons by his two wives, Nang Yomphala and Nang Et-khaeng. Then he found seven beautiful princesses to marry his sons. After that he taught them how to rule the kingdom peacefully. He also taught his daughters-in-law how to be good queens and housewives. Then he distributed all kinds of treasures to his seven sons and allocated noblemen and ministers to help them rule their new cities.

Khoun Bulom sent his seven sons to rule various cities. Khoun Lo was sent to Chawa, Lan Xang (today called Luang Phra Bang); Yi Muang Phalan went to Nongsae; Jungsawang was sent to Muang Kaewluang (Muang Phakan); Saiphong was sent to Muang Yuanyao; Ngou-In went to Muang Sidayothaya; Lokkom went to Xiangkhom (Khamkao or Khamkoed;) and Jetcheuang was sent to Muang Phuan.*

Before the sons traveled to their cities, Khoun Bulom taught them an important message. "Each of you must not mistreat the others. Each must attend to his own city. Do not ever invade the other's city. You must follow our ancient kingly rules. Elder brothers, you are already prosperous. You must not be greedy, trying to take over your younger brothers' cities. It you do that, you will face all kinds of misfortune in the future. As for the younger brothers, I bless you with prosperity. You must keep your older brothers informed of your well-being. If anything or anyone, belonging to the other, comes to you, you must return it to the owner. Do not ever appropriate anything that is not your own."

So his teaching went on to cover all topics necessary for all cities to live in peace and harmony, while the sons listened attentively. Khoun Bulom continued ruling the city, setting down all kinds of law and order, which later became Khoun Bulom's Law (*kod mai thammasat khun bulom*). Not long after that, Khoun Bulom died and his sons held a royal funeral, befitting the great king. After the two queens died, the seven brothers took an oath to be friends. They left to rule their own assigned cities.

With that the story of Khoun Bulom ends.

---

*Legends disagree about which cities the brothers were sent to. One even has Lokkom being sent to Muang Hongsawadee in Burma.

KHUA KHAO KAAD: THE GIANT CREEPER

From *Kheu Khao Kaad* by Souban Luanglahd. Retold by Wajuppa Tossa.

This is another myth about the problems the earth faced with growth of the giant vine: how the greatest god, Thaen, sent the first couple down to earth to get rid of the creeper; how that couple sacrificed their lives to do so; and about the annual ritual humans must observe to express gratitude to this ancient couple.

Phya Thaen sent one of his sons, named Khoun Bulom, to be born on the human world. Khoun Bulom gathered all the people and led them to establish a city in a land called Na Noi Oy Nu (area of present-day northern Laos and Dien Bien Phu, Vietnam). The king ruled the city for a long time, but the people were poor. So they begged Phya Thaen for help.

Phya Thaen looked over the city with his divine eyes and saw the giant creeper called *Khua Khao Kaad,* whose vine was huge and long. It crept up from earth to heaven. The branches and leaves of the creeper were so huge that they blocked the sunlight, which in turn prevented the people from getting good crops from their agriculture. Besides, the vine became a path for supernatural beings and spirits of the dead to come to the human world.

Seeing this, Phya Thaen sent an old married couple called Pu Mod and Ya Ngam to the human world. The couple led the people to make a living for a long time, but everyone was still as poor as ever. The people gathered for consultation and unanimously agreed that, "The cause of all the poverty and hardship comes from the giant creeper. We must have it cut."

Actually, the cutting of the giant creeper was very complicated. The cutter would be killed in cutting the vine. Pu Mod and Ya Ngam realized that they had been sent to earth by Phya Thaen to help the people. Thus, they felt ready to sacrifice their lives for the well-being of everyone on earth.

Before attempting to cut the vine, the couple gave their last word: "After we are dead, if you have meat, you must send some to us with the crow. If you have fish, you must send some to us with the vulture." Then the old couple began cutting the vine. They worked without stop day and night until all their energy was spent. But at last they had managed to cut down the horrid vine that was blocking the sun.

Now to express their gratitude and to thank Pu Mod and Ya Ngam, the people make merit and dedicate it to the old couple every year.

The ancient couple are also known as Pu Nyoe and Ya Nyoe. It is said that Pu Nyoe told the people to remember his sacrifice in cutting the giant vine by calling out his name, "Nyoe." So this word "Nyoe," appears at the end of many phrases in Lao, such as Ma Nyoe *(Come here),* Non Nyoe *(Go to sleep), and* Kin Nyoe *(Eat).*

A special ceremony for Pu Nyoe and Ya Nyoe is held on the eighth day of the sixth lunar month. Life-sized puppets representing the couple dance and a lion figure dances behind them. A story tells that the couple caught a lion in the Himavanta Forest. They raised the lion as their adopted son. And the lion became their guardian. It is believed that this lion had been terrorizing the Luang Phabang area, so the couple are honored for taming the beast.

The couple are also honored during the Lao New Year's celebrations, when the puppets may lead processions, dancing. Some versions of the myth tell that these mythical persons made the earth by stamping on the immense ocean that covered the world. They then planted gourd seeds and from these the first men appeared. In other versions they were sent from heaven to cut down the giant vine.

THE FOUR MARVELOUS BROTHERS: A FOLKTALE OF THE LAO PHUAN PEOPLE

Retold by Kongdeuane Nettavong. Translated by Wajuppa Tossa.

This story tells of the origin of the Lao Phuan people.

*O*nce upon a time, there was a childless old couple who lived near the river bank at the foot of a high mountain. The couple had been poor ever since they were married. The couple wished to have children to help them work and to continue their lineage. Other families near them enjoyed having children around. Those with children could travel here and there easily. For this poor old couple, they could not enjoy such pleasure. Even when they became exhausted, they could not afford to stop working. They had to work to earn their living.

The poor couple consulted with each other one day: "We should go to ask for blessings from the *devata* guarding the high mountain. Perhaps we may have a meritorious child who is diligent and may be a great help to us in farming. He can look after us when we get sick or take care of our properties after we have passed on. Then, we can be like others in our village."

The couple prepared flowers, candles, and incense sticks to go ask for a child as their wish. The two raised their hands, palms together in a prayer position, and together they spoke: "Sathu, sathu, we are so poor and suffering. May the great *devata* bestow a great blessing on us. May we be granted a child of our own."

On the way home, an unusual incident occurred. It so frightened them that they both turned pale. When they looked up in the sky, they saw a giant dragon blowing multicolored rays of fire down onto a bush right in front of them.

The old couple thought, "There must be something magical happening there." After the dragon disappeared in the clouds, they rushed to look at the bush. There they saw a golden pumpkin, a silver squash, one black grain (a sesame seed), and one white grain (rice), shining like diamonds and jewels. They carefully wrapped these things in a *phakhawma*, the all-purpose cloth, and returned home.

Once home, the couple did not know where to properly put those things. "How about putting them in a corner of the hut?" asked the husband. "Oh, no, they might get soiled," said the wife. "How about putting them in a jar?" asked the wife. "Oh, no, that might be too stuffy," said the husband. Then the husband had an idea. "I will weave a bamboo cradle and hang it in the middle of the room. What do you think, wife?" The wife agreed, "That's a good idea. We could put our children in the cradle and rock them back and forth." They called their treasures their "children." The husband then began weaving the cradle. Once it was done, he hung the cradle in the middle of the room and said to his wife, "Now we must take very good care of our children." And so they did. They loved their "children" as much as their own eyes.

Days and nights went by, and the golden pumpkin, the silver squash, the rice grain, and the sesame seed grew unusually large and heavy. The old couple could no longer lift them. The wife could only rock the cradle back and forth, taking very good care of them as if they were their own children.

Ever since they had been in possession of the four things, the old man had become stronger and more diligent. He went to work on his farm more regularly. Each day the old man would clear the entire mountain for farming, without feeling tired. Each day he would plant his crops, without the least fatigue. Each day, the old man would see more and more of the lush squashes, pumpkins, sesame seeds, and rice grains. He could not believe his own eyes, and each day he would say in awe, "Look at all those crops. I can't possibly do all that by myself! That is the work of a hundred strong men."

The old man came to tell his wife about what he saw. Both of them became amazed and puzzled. That night the couple made a plan. They went to bed earlier than usual so that they could wake up at night to watch their "children." Late at night, as the couple were hiding and watching the cradle, they became astounded and speechless. They saw four handsome young lads hatching out of the golden pumpkin, the silver squash, the rice grain, and the sesame seed. The lads were carrying farming tools in their hands. The four young men then left the hut. The couple hurried to hide the shells of the golden pumpkin, the silver squash, the rice grain, and the sesame seed before tracing the four young men's tracks. They wondered what they could be doing in the middle of the night. Once they reached the farm, they saw the four young men digging the earth, making vegetable beds, and planting something at great speed. It seemed as if they were using magic.

As the dawn was approaching and the roosters began to crow, the four hurriedly walked home. Once home, they could not find their shells. They began searching for them, but in vain. Then they began to discuss and reason. The old couple came out of hiding and said to them, "My sons, don't feel upset about this. You can live keeping your human forms and continue living with us. We love you so much." The four young men replied, "Dear Father, Dear Mother, if you so love us, please allow us to live in our shells until the proper time has come. We shall turn into complete human beings on the full moon night of the twelfth lunar month." The old couple listened in awe. "On that day, you must prepare a tray of flowers, candles, and incense sticks to present to the shells to pay homage to them on our behalf. Once we are out of the shells, we should continue doing homage to the shells on the same day each year. Then, the shells will become magic and good for healing all kinds of sickness." After so saying, the four young lads said good-bye and returned to live inside their shells again.

On the full moon night of the twelfth lunar month, the old couple followed the young men's instructions. They prepared a tray with flowers, candles, and incense to honor the shells. The young men stepped out of their shells and bowed to their parents. "Now we can live with you and be your children."

The young men continued living and taking care of the couple happily until they reached the age of eighteen. Then the sons begged their mother to carry the golden pumpkin, the silver squash, the white rice, and the black sesame seed to offer as gifts to the kings of each of four different cities. They were to ask for the hand in marriage of the daughter of each king. When the kings of these cities saw what had been sent to them, they were delighted and were more than happy to grant the old woman's request.

The sons then became royal son-in-laws. Each son inherited part of the kingdom together with subjects to be under his care. The golden pumpkin prince became Phya Muang Lum or king of the lowland, whose protectorate covered lands along the Ngiew River. The silver squash prince became Phya Muang Fa, king of the great high mountains. The black sesame seed prince became Phya Muang Thoeng, king of the highlands which are Phu Xuang, Phu Saed, and Phu Daedka. The white rice prince became Phya Sipsong Hou Muang, king of the twelve areas.

After the four brothers went to rule the four cities, the shells of the golden pumpkin, the silver squash, the rice grain, and the sesame seed became mines of gold, silver, gems, and jewels spreading all over the lands. Thus their subjects, who were commoners, could use those precious things for their ornaments.

When farming season began, the kings came to help their people work in the fields and farms. Everyone was helping each other year in and year out, until it became a custom for the people to lend a helping hand in farming. Thus each city became prosperous, with granaries filled with rice; ponds filled with fish; and farms filled with pumpkins, squashes, sesame plants, and rice of all kinds and colors, the black rice, the red rice, and the brown rice.

As time went by, the four kings led their people to build their cities to become prosperous, with contented subjects. The old couple went to visit their sons' families and grandchildren alternately. They led the people in the rite of paying homage to the shells of the pumpkins, squashes, rice, and sesame seeds after the harvest was done, on the full moon day in the twelfth lunar month.

Since then, Lao people from some areas will hold a merit making ceremony after harvest each year. They believe that by having such a ceremony, the spirits of their deceased ancestors and relatives will receive the merit and will be contented and peaceful. The offerings in these ceremonies often include pumpkins, squashes, sesame seed bags, sticky rice and sesame seeds, sesame rice chips, rice grains, cooked rice, and popped-rice. When people fall ill, they mix dried shells of pumpkins, squashes, rice grains, and sesame seeds with other ingredients to make medicine for healing, as they were taught by the four brothers in the myth.

THE ORIGIN OF THE MEKONG RIVER

Retold by Wajuppa Tossa.

The Lao people say that the Mekong River originated from Nong Kasae and that the water from the Mekong and the Nan River can never mix. If they are put together in a bottle, that bottle will burst. This origin story is told as part of the epic of Phadaeng Nang Ai. See Part XII for more of that story.

Once upon a time there lived two dragon kings in Nong Kasae. One dragon was called Souttoranark (King Soutto), and the other dragon was Souvanranark (King Souvan). Each was very powerful and had many thousands of followers. They became good friends. Every year they visited and helped one another in many ways, often exchanging gifts. One day King Soutto and his men went into a forest to hunt. He was lucky to find big game, an elephant. In spite of its thin hair, the elephant is one of the largest animals. King Soutto gave a big share of the meat to his friend. When King Souvan received the gift, he was delighted and sent back a message to thank his friend.

One day in the third month, King Souvan and his soldiers went out to hunt along the lake. They were making a determined effort to find big game such as deer, rhinoceros, elephant, or buffalo, but they did not have any luck. They could not find anything. Finally the king managed to get a porcupine. He and his people returned to the palace and skinned and cut up the animal. Then the king divided the meat into equal parts. Souvan had his men take Soutto's share to him. Seeing that the skin and the spines of the animal were beautiful, the king sent some of them along, too. When King Soutto looked at the amount of meat in comparison with the spines, he thought that his friend was unfair. He thought the spines of the porcupine were the "hairs" of the animal and assumed it must be a very large creature. "How could he possibly do that to me?" he thought. "Only this much meat from the biggest animal in the world ? I can't believe it," he said. He refused to accept the gift and told his friend's soldiers to return the gift. He also told them to ask their king to come to see him personally. But before leaving, King Souvan's soldiers pleaded, "Your Majesty, this is the meat of a porcupine. Although its spines are much larger than elephant hair, its body itself is much smaller than an elephant. That is why we could bring only this much meat."

King Soutto was still very angry and would not listen. Upon their arrival at King Souvan's palace, the men went straight to report the incident. "Your Majesty," they said, "your gift that we delivered has been refused. King Soutto also told us to ask you to come to see him tomorrow."

King Souvanranark, after hearing that, said, "What has become of my dear friend? I'm going to find out myself tomorrow. In any case, I don't think he is going to give up. I don't think he will listen to my explanation. And I don't think he knows what a porcupine is. He just looked at its spines and thought it was an animal bigger than an elephant. Why doesn't he see that what I gave was a sincere gift? Even though it was just a small amount, it was an equal share. I didn't take advantage of him. Why did he return it to me with anger instead of thanks?"

At dawn the following morning, the dragon, King Soutto, assembled all his men in the meeting hall, thinking his friend would come. When all his men reported to him, Soutto spoke to them with a firm voice, "We should be prepared, because our friend Souvan has betrayed us. He did not follow our agreement. He will come to settle the problem with me by himself. All of you know that a porcupine is a larger animal than an elephant because its spines are so big and sharp, it must be the largest animal in the world."

After his ministers heard that, they thought they should explain to the king which animal was larger, but they were afraid of being executed. Instead, they kept quiet and said, "We are ready to listen to your order, Your Majesty."

At that moment, the dragon king, Souvan, and his people appeared. Even though King Soutto was still angry, he gave his friend a warm welcome. But he thought he wouldn't excuse Souvan, if he did not admit that he was guilty. As soon as the meeting opened, Soutto began speaking, "Dear friend Souvan, I thought we were really sincere friends and both would follow our agreement seriously. I don't see how you could betray me."

Souvan denied his friend's accusation of being dishonest. He said that he loved and trusted his friend. He could swear for his faithfulness. These statements made Soutto even more furious, and he said he could not listen. He invited comments from the audience.

He asked, "Which of us is selfish or inconsiderate? When I got an elephant, a smaller animal than a porcupine, I gave my friend an equal share, while he gave me only a small amount of the porcupine meat. That was not fair."

When Soutto finished talking, his soldiers applauded him and laughed at King Souvan. When the noise faded away, Souvan explained again, "Please listen again, my dear friend. I don't think you have ever seen a porcupine. You cannot judge the size of an animal by the size of its spines or hair. An elephant is a big animal but its hair is very thin. Even its eyes are small. The eyes of other animals, such as buffaloes, cows, and horses, are larger than an elephant's, but their bodies are smaller. Of course, a porcupine's spine is larger than the hair of an elephant, but its body is not much larger than some kinds of birds. Please don't misunderstand. Don't break our friendship. Please think that I am always your good friend and I also think that you are always my best friend."

No matter what and how much Souvan tried to explain, Soutto insisted that what his friend said was not true. He rose from his chair and walked away. Souvan left without knowing what was going to happen next.

A few days later, King Soutto sent a message to King Souvan saying that if Souvan was still stubborn he should prepare for an attack. After reading the message, Souvan realized that he had no choice. He immediately sounded the gong to assemble his men. When they gathered they discussed how ignorant and inconsiderate Soutto was.

Seven days after the message reached Souvan, the angry dragon, Soutto, moved his force to Souvan's territory. All the dragons have magic power. They moved so fast that they churned the water until it was muddy. Suddenly, Souvan ordered his soldiers to confront them, causing a big turmoil. All the Kuva area became cloudy and hazy. The sun could not be seen for seven days. All the animals, big and small, were afraid. The birds flew away. The war went on and on, for the two sides were equally strong. The water became muddier. More and more living beings were dying, and chaos forced some of the gods living in the heavens to move away. Indra, the king of gods, sympathized with the small animals, so he cast a spell with his supernatural power to threaten the two friends. Finally they stopped fighting.

Indra ordered them to build two rivers to compensate for their deeds. Soutto was responsible for making the Mekong run from the lake to the sea, while Souvan was put in charge of building the Nan River. The god finally convinced Soutto that a porcupine really was a small animal and made him understand Souvan. Ever after they were good friends again.

But the waters of the two rivers have not yet forgotten the hatred that led to their creation. To this day they say that if you put water from both the Mekong and the Nan Rivers into a single container, the container will shatter!

PART 12

Folk Epics

Here we present heroic figures of the Lao people. One hero, Khun Bulomrajathirat, more often called Khun Bulom, was supposed to be the first human king sent from heaven to lead the Lao people to prosperity. His story is told in Part 11 along with other myths of the origin of the Lao people.

A second legendary hero in Laos is Thao Hung Thao Cheuang, who is supposed to have left concrete objects as a reminder: gigantic jars made of solid stone. These jars of various sizes were scattered over the vast plateau in Xiang Khuang region outside of Phonsavanh district. This area is called The Plain of Jars, Thong Hai Hin. They are an archeological mystery. The jars are estimated to be at least 2,000 years old. This mystery is by no means a mystery to the Lao people, as they believe that these gigantic jars are whiskey or wine jars of their great Khmer king, Thao Cheuang. Thao Hung Thao Cheuang is a hero of the Lao people, as well as of peoples in various other countries in Southeast Asia. The settings of his story cover a wide area: present-day northern Thailand, Laos, Vietnam, and Burma. Versions and variations of the story exist in Laos, Vietnam, and northern Thailand. Each version shares the same plot structure, with varying details in the middle and at the end. Only summaries of the story are presented here, due to the length of the epic.

Two other folk epics are introduced here: *Phya Khankhaak, the Toad King* and *Phadaeng Nang Ai (King Phadaeng and Princess Aikham)*. A similar version of the story in Laos is called *The White Squirrel (Ka Hog Don)*. The two epics we give here are retold from versions known in Isaan, Northeastern Thailand. Variants told in Laos differ in details. The *bun bangfai* (the rocket festival) is an important annual event in Isaan and Laos. Fireworks are shot into the heavens to remind Phya Thaen to send rain, just as he instructed the people to do in the story *Phya Khankhaak*. The full versions of *Phadaeng Nang Ai* and *Phya Khankhaak, the Toad King* have been translated into English by Dr. Wajuppa Tossa and are accessible through libraries.

These folk epics are complicated. *Phadaeng Nang Ai* relies heavily on the Buddhist concept of rebirth. The same characters reappear as different people in the various episodes. The lengthy epic of Thao Hung Thao Cheuang is barely sketched out here and yet is quite confusing, with its many unusual names for characters and places. We include these epics here in brief, because they play such an important part in the cultural life of Lao people in both Isaan and Laos.

PHYA KHANKHAAK, THE TOAD KING

Transcription of palm leaf manuscript by Phra Ariyanuwat Khemajari. Retold by Wajuppa Tossa.

*O*nce, long ago, there was a prosperous kingdom ruled by King Ekthita and Queen Sida. After a long time, the queen conceived. The court astrologer predicted that the prince would be most meritorious and powerful. Everyone was waiting to behold this infant with high hopes. Ten lunar months went by and the queen was in labor.

The royal midwife looked at the royal infant and was shocked. She silenced the servants, "Don't say a word about the fact that this royal infant looks like a toad."

And so no one uttered a word. But when the royal infant was presented to the king, he cried with joy. "Oh, my royal meritorious son, you do look like a toad. But I love you. Look at your complexion, it is golden."

"I proclaim the name of my royal son to be 'Khankhaak Kuman' or 'The Toad Prince, Khankhaak'." And that's the name of our hero. Everyone loved the toad prince. He was such a delightful fellow. When he grew up to be a young prince, he went to his royal father.

"Father, I am old enough to be married. I wish to have a castle of ten thousand pillars and one thousand rooms decorated with gems and jewels. And I wish to have the most beautiful maiden as my wife."

"Son, I could have the castle built for you, but to ask for a hand of any beautiful woman to be your wife might not be possible. You look like a toad, my dear son," said his father.

The young prince was full of disappointment and returned to his palace, contemplating what to do. Then he thought of Indra, the highest god in heaven. He put his hands together and prayed to Indra.

"Oh, Dear Indra, please help to fulfill my wish, for my father could not do so for me."

After making that wish he went to sleep. He slept so soundly that he hardly knew what happened that night. Indra came to bless him and bestowed everything that he had wished for. When he woke up, he was in the most splendid castle of ten thousand pillars and one thousand rooms decorated with gems and jewels. He peeled off his toadlike form and was turned into the most handsome prince. When he looked beside him, there was a heavenly maid.

"Oh, are you a human or a celestial being?" asked the toad prince.

"I am a human princess from the northern hemisphere. Indra brought me here to be your wife, my lord. My name is Nang Kaew-udon," replied the mysterious lady.

And so they talked and got to know each other. They became husband and wife that very night.

The next day, the entire court was greatly startled by the appearance of the new castle. They informed the king and queen about this. So the king went to the toad prince's palace. With amazement and awe, he saw a handsome prince and a beautiful maiden in this splendid castle. Once he learned that it was his own toad prince son, he relinquished the throne to his son and his daughter-in-law. The toad prince now was entitled "Phya Khankhaak, the Toad King." He ruled the city with compassion and generosity. The kind and generous queen Nang Kaew-udon contributed to his fame as the most meritorious king by setting up food pavilions for the poor.

Not long after that, the fame of this king and queen spread throughout the earth and the universe. Human kings, celestial beings, demi-celestial creatures endowed with magical power like the *naga* (a mythical serpent in Buddhist cosmology), *garuda* (a mythical creature, half-bird and half-man), demons, animals, and insects came to pay respects and homage to him. They came with tributes and emissaries to present to the king and queen. Not one single creature remembered to hold a ceremony to pay tribute to the rain god, Phya Thaen.

Phya Thaen was so humiliated that he did not permit the *naga* to play in the heavenly lakes to make rain for the earthlings. Horrible fires broke out in every forest. All this happened outside the palace walls, so the king and queen had no knowledge of this catastrophe. After seven years, seven months, and seven days, the subjects of Phya Khankhaak came to ask for help. Phya Khankhaak went to visit the Naga King to find out the cause of this disastrous drought. Like most Thai-Lao people, Phya Khankhaak believed that the *naga*'s bathing, playing, and tail lashing in Phya Thaen's lake in heaven was the origin of rain on earth. Once he learned that Phya Thaen refused to let the *naga* play in the heavenly lake, Phya Khankhaak organized a great army of all humans, animals, insects, demons, and celestial beings to go to heaven to fight Phya Thaen. Once the bridge between heaven and earth was created, with the help of all creatures, they marched up to heaven singing their marching song:

Oh, oh, What a woe!   Thaen has been our foe,
For he refused   to bestow rain to earth.
Come one, come all;   let us go to fight Thaen.
From that crowd come   wasps, hornets, and bees.
Those beautiful creatures   are deer with bright eyes.
Those with golden bodies   are beautiful celestial beings or *thewada*.
This crowd of beings   are frogs and toads of all kinds.
Those dignified animals   are *garuda*, *naga*, and lions.

Oh, oh, what a woe!	Thaen has been our foe,
For he refused	to bestow rain to earth.
Come one come all;	Let us go to fight Thaen.
Those approaching are	wood mites, termites, dogs and bears.
And these are	eagles, porcupines, civet cats, and tigers.
Those splendid creatures	are pheasants and swans.
Those cheerful creatures are	apes, monkeys, elephants and horses.
Those in the front row	are flying lemurs and cuckoo birds.
Oh, oh, What a woe!	Thaen has been our foe,
For he refused	to bestow rain to earth.
Come one come all;	let us go to fight Thaen.

And so the battle began. After a long, perilous, and miraculous battle, Phya Khankhaak won. He then taught Phya Thaen to be just and to bestow rain on the universe seasonally.

"You must promise to send rain to earth when the rice planting season comes," ordered Phya Khankhaak, the Toad King.

"Yes, I promise. However, if I forget, I would like the humans to send up rockets to remind me of the appropriate time to send rains. Then I will call the *naga* to come play in the heavenly lake to make rain for the earthlings."

"So, let that become our customary rite for fertility. We will have the rocket festival when there is no sign of rain in the rice planting season," said Phya Khankhaak, the Toad King.

After enjoying Phya Thaen's heaven for a few months, Phya Khankhaak came back to rule the fertile earth happily. Every once in a while, Phya Khankhaak would recount the story of how he led a great army to fight Phya Thaen and how he enjoyed spending some time in heaven after his victory.

Note: It is believed that Phya Khankaak was one of the past lives of the historical Buddha. Eventually he was reborn as the historical Buddha, and his wife and relatives were reborn as people in the historical Buddha's lifetime.

PHADAENG NANG AI

Transcription of palm leaf manuscript by Phra Ariyanuwat Khemajari. Retold by Wajuppa Tossa.

The story of Phadaeng Nang Ai is a complicated one, as there are many subplots that would give the reader background on how the story develops. To understand the main plot, the reader needs to understand two particular scenes from the past life of the major characters—Nang Aikham's and Phangkhi's past lives, and the story of Phangkhi's father. This tale is the version told in Isaan, Northeastern Thailand. At one time the Khmer Kingdom spread across much of this area, hence the mention here of Khmer kings.

Part 1: Princess Aikham or Nang Ai's Past Life as Nang Amkha and the Naga Prince Phangkhi's Past Life as a Mute

*O*nce there was a rich man who had a beautiful daughter named Nang Amkha. The rich man wished to have a kind and industrious man as his son-in-law. Nang Amkha herself was not interested in any young man in the same village. Now in a faraway village there was a young man who was a beggar. He wandered from his village begging for his daily living. One day he appeared at the rich man's door, begging for food.

"What can I do for you, young man?" asked the rich man.

The young man placed one hand on his stomach and the other to his mouth.

"Oh, you are hungry," said the rich man. "Why don't you say so?"

The young man pointed to his mouth and waved his hands, shaking his head.

"Oh, you cannot speak," said the rich man. "That is quite all right. Will someone bring this man food?" ordered the rich man.

When the young man finished eating, he put his hands together in a praying position as a sign of thanks.

"You are quite welcome, young man. It's already dark. Why don't you stay here?" offered the rich man.

The young man smiled and thanked the rich man again. He was led to his sleeping quarters. The next day, he woke up and began working. He swept the yard, trimmed the overgrown trees, and fetched water to fill all the jars.

The rich man woke up just in time to see how the young man worked so diligently.

"This is a promising young man even though he cannot speak. I like him." thought the rich man. He went to the young man and said, "Young man, you did a good job. Would you like to stay and work for me?" The young man smiled and nodded his head in acceptance of the offer. He stayed with the rich man for a long time, working hard on every chore around the house. The rich man grew so fond of the mute man that he made it clear to all that they must treat the mute man as his own son. Several times the mute man came and made gestures showing his intention of leaving, but the rich man would convince him to stay a little longer every time. The rich man kept thinking of how he could keep the young man with him. One day he had an idea. He called his daughter, Nang Amkha, and the young man to see him.

"Now Nang Amkha, you are old enough to be married. Do you have someone in mind?" asked the old man.

"Oh, no, Father, I have no one and I wish to be with you forever. If I am married, I have to go and stay at my husband's house. Please don't send me away so soon, Father," begged Nang Amkha.

"How about you, my dear young man? You are also old enough to have a family. Do you have someone in mind?" asked the rich man.

The young man shook his head in answer to that question. The rich man was hopeful. He smiled and said, "Ah, then you two can be married. You can stay with me and Nang Amkha does not have to go elsewhere."

Nang Amkha blushed and looked down at the floor, for she also had grown a fond feeling toward the young man. The young man rose and went to sit beside her in acceptance of the rich man's offer.

And so they were married according to the customary rite. The first night of the wedding, when the ceremony of sending the bride and groom to the bedroom was over, the rich man left his daughter in the room with her future husband. Once the parent was out of sight, the young man walked out of the room to sleep in another room.

"Oh, you wished to stay in your old room, then. I can go to be with you there," said Nang Amkha. She followed him to his room. Again, the young man left the room to go back to the wedding room. She followed him again, but he left and went back to his old room.

"He must not want me to be with him, then," said the bride. "Then I will just stay here by myself."

Nang Amkha treated her husband with respect, without letting anyone know how he treated her. After many years of marriage, the young man came to gesture to the rich man that he wished to return home to visit his parents in a faraway city by himself, but the rich man asked him to take his wife along so that she could meet her in-laws. Nang Amkha prepared a lot of food supplies for the journey. She carried them on her shoulders and followed her husband, who walked ahead, clearing the way with his sword. They went on and on for many days and nights without a sign of being near his village. They went on and on until they had consumed all of the food supplies. They went deeper and deeper in the jungle until they came across a fig tree with red ripe fruit on the top branches.

The young man pointed up to the top branches and quickly climbed up. Nang Amkha waited and waited, feeling hungrier and hungrier, but there was no sign that her husband would climb down and share the ripe figs with her.

"Oh, I have to try to climb the tree myself for the fruit. I am so hungry." After saying that, she climbed up to one of the branches and quenched her hunger with the ripe fruit. When she felt a little better, she looked around. Her husband was nowhere to be seen.

"He may be at the pond, drinking water or bathing. I will climb down and see," said the young wife.

"Husband, husband, where are you?" she called out, but there was no answer. She walked around and around, but in vain. It was getting darker and darker and the jungle sounds became scarier and scarier.

Hopeless, the young wife went to drink water and bathe in a pond nearby. As she was sitting and thinking about her life as a deserted wife, she became overwhelmed with fury.

She put her hands together in a praying position and made a final wish.

"In my next life, I wish for revenge on my negligent husband. In this life, my husband abandoned me amid the wild forest; in my next incarnation, may retribution befall him. In his next life, I wish him to die in a high branch of a tree; I vow that he will never be my husband again."

She died in the forest with a broken heart. In her next lives, she was born and was married to her husband, but in each of these lives, she paid no attention to him. He died of a broken heart in all of those lives. In the most recent incarnation, Nang Amkha was born as a Khmer princess, Nang Aikham, and her husband was born as a *naga* prince, Phangkhi.

Part 2: Phangkhi's Father, Soutto Naga King

The mute man was now reborn as the *naga* prince Phangkhi. He was the one and only son of King Soutto Naga of the Mekong River. Before Soutto Naga King ruled the Mekong River, he was in Nongsae, the river in the northern hemisphere, sharing the kingdom with his beloved friend, Souvan Naga. They lived in peace and harmony, sharing whatever they could find, particularly food.

One day Soutto Naga found an elephant for food; he sent a half portion of the meat to his friend, Souvan Naga. It was a huge portion indeed. This kind of sharing went on and on, and nothing happened until one day Souvan Naga caught a porcupine. He sent half of the find to his friend, Soutto Naga. When Soutto Naga saw the small portion of the meat, he was infuriated, thinking that the porcupine was a huge animal judging from its long spines. He thought the size of the meat depended on the size of the hair of the animal. Thus, since the spines of the porcupine were so long, the meat should be much more than that of the elephant.

Soutto Naga sent back the portion of the porcupine meat to Souvan Naga, who then went to visit Soutto Naga. He did not understand why his friend would return the share of meat. Once there, he tried to explain to Soutto Naga, but Soutto Naga refused to listen and chased Souvan Naga home. On returning home, Souvan Naga envisioned an attack from his friend, so he closed the gate, preparing to defend his city. Souvan Naga was right. Soutto Naga became more aggravated after his friend left him. He organized an army and went to attack Souvan Naga's city. They fought for a long time, but no one won. Many *naga* were killed, until the river became muddy and bloody. The cloud of dust rose to heaven along with the loud rumbling noises of the battle.

Their fight caused a lot of trouble for all water and land creatures as well as the celestial beings in that area. Indra sent his celestial being down to stop the fight and judged the case. After hearing the root cause of the great battle, the celestial being ordered Souvan Naga to create a river from one side of the Nongsae Lake until he reached the sea and then to rule the area called the Nan River (which runs from the north to the Chao Phya River and to the gulf of Siam). As for Soutto Naga, he must create a river from the other side of the Nongsae until he reached the sea and rule the area called the Mekong River. And that was the story of Soutto Naga, the father of the young *naga* prince, Phangkhi.

Part 3: Nang Aikham and Phadaeng

There was once a prosperous and powerful Khmer kingdom ruled by Phya Khom and his queen, Nang Chan. They had a daughter, whose beauty was renowned in all lands, including the land of the *naga*. It was the highest dream of all to be able to get a glimpse of this divine princess, Nang Aikham.

King Phadaeng of Phaphong city also heard of the beauty of Nang Aikham. He mounted his favorite horse and went on his way to see Nang Aikham. Bak Sam, his favorite servant, went with him on this journey, preparing all kinds of gifts to present to the princess. After a long journey they came to the outskirts of Nang Aikham's city.

King Phadaeng and his servant met with Nang Aikham's servants outside the city. He sent his gifts to be presented to the princess and asked to have an audience with her. Once Nang Aikham saw the gifts, she was overjoyed. She sent gifts of monk's robes and *naga* design cloths as well as a set of betel and areca nut to Phadaeng as her token of friendship.

Phadaeng readily accepted the gifts. After chewing the betel and areca nut, he put on the *naga* design cloth and wore it to have an audience with Nang Aikham. Once there, the princess welcomed him to her chamber. They spent the entire day together. She offered him dinner, betel, and areca nut. They stayed together, courting with loving words until it was dawn. Phadaeng bade Nang Aikham goodbye, promising to return to her. "My beloved lady, please wait for me to return." He left her to be sad and lonely, longing to see him.

They did not have to wait long. When the sixth lunar month arrived, Nang Ai's father, Phya Khom, organized a *bun bangfai* (rocket) festival to provoke the rain god, Phya Thaen, to send rain to earth. He invited all kings to bring the processions of rockets to shoot in the festival. Many kings from many lands prepared their locally made rockets to join the festival. Phya Khom also set a prize for the winner to rule half of his kingdom and to be married to his beautiful daughter, Nang Aikham. The winner must be able to shoot the rocket straight up to the sky, and it must stay up for the longest time. However, if Phya Khom's rocket was the winner, he would be given all kinds of tributary gifts from all contestants in the festival.

Phadaeng was not invited, but he came to join the festival, hoping to win the contest and the heart of his beloved Nang Aikham. In this way, they could be married according to the customary rite.

When all the kings came to pay respect to Phya Khom, he was delighted to have many contestants in the festival. Phya Khom was particularly impressed with Phadaeng's rocket and his charismatic persona. He secretly wished to have Phadaeng as his son-in-law. The celebration went on for seven days and seven nights. During this time, Phadaeng had chances to be with Nang Aikham again and to renew their love ties.

Part 4: The *Bangfai* Contest

After the celebration was over, the contest of the rocket shooting began. The rockets from the cities of Fadaed, Sikaew, Chianghian, and Muanghongmuangthong went up straight and high. Phadaeng's rocket exploded at the launcher. He was so humiliated that he could not wait to hear the result of the contest. He gathered his procession, bade farewell to Nang Aikham, and returned to his home city in Phaphong. Phya Khom's rocket failed to ignite. Like Phadaeng, Phya Khom felt so humiliated and angered that he refused to keep his promise. He sent all the kings home without granting any prizes to them.

Part 5: Phangkhi, Nang Aikham, and Phadaeng— The Tragic Ending

Because the *naga* prince, Phangkhi, and Nang Aikham had been husband and wife in their past lives, they were destined to meet each other again. Like other young men, Phangkhi had also heard about the beauty of Nang Aikham the Khmer princess. The strong tie in the past life led him to travel to the human world to see Nang Aikham. He transformed himself and his *naga* servants by magic to become handsome young men attending the *bangfai* festival and to try to get a glimpse of the beautiful Nang Aikham. Seeing her from afar, Phangkhi fell deeply in love with Nang Aikham. After the rocket festival was over, he remained in the city, trying to find ways to be near Nang Aikham. He disguised himself as a white squirrel wearing a golden bell around his neck. He climbed the fig tree near Nang Aikham's palace so she could see him. The musical sounds of his bell alerted Nang Aikham to come out and look at him. Again, because of the tie from the past life, she loved that white squirrel and wished to have him as her pet.

She went to see the court hunter and ordered him to catch the white squirrel for her. But because of her final wish in the past life, she made a slip and implied that the hunter should use a poisoned arrow to shoot the squirrel. The hunter shot down the white squirrel with the poison arrow. Once he was shot, Phangkhi ordered his *naga* servants to return to the *naga* city and to inform his father, Soutto Naga, of what had happened. Before the poison reached his heart, he made a dying wish. He wished that his meat become endlessly abundant, aromatic, and delicious when he was sliced up as the Khmer people's food.

After his death, the Khmer people from all over the land came to take a share. No one could resist the aromatic, succulent, and juicy meat. Phya Khom, the king, distributed the meat to all of his people, except for the widows. Every one enjoyed the meat of Phangkhi, even the Khmer king's royal family, particularly Nang Aikham.

Once Soutto Naga King heard the news of his son's death, he gathered his *naga* army to take revenge for his son. He followed the aroma of the squirrel's meat. He destroyed the entire Khmer kingdom, except for the widows' houses, which became an island in the middle of the great lake.

At that time, Phadaeng, hearing of the catastrophe, came riding his horse to Nang Aikham's palace and took her on his horseback to escape Soutto Naga King's wrath. As they were riding out of the city, Soutto Naga King followed close behind. Nang Aikham carried all the royal regalia with her in preparation for setting up a new kingdom.

Soutto Naga King followed her so closely that she had to throw the regalia away one by one. The place where she threw the gong is now called Huay Namkhong, the place where she threw the drum is called Huay Kongsii, and the place where she threw her ring is called Nong Waen. However, even after she threw all the regalia away, Soutto Naga King still followed her. Finally, he got hold of her and dragged her down underwater to the *naga* city. After Phadaeng died, he became the Ghost King and raised an army to fight to get Nang Aikham back from the *naga* city. They fought for a long time, and no one could win. Finally the supreme god, Indra, came to stop the fight. He sent Phadaeng back to the ghost city and ordered Nang Aikham to stay in the *naga* city, waiting for the arrival of the next Buddha in the Buddhist Era of 5000. It is now B.E. 2550. According to the story, the next Buddha will make the final judgment of whom Nang Aikham should be with.

THAO HUNG THAO CHEUANG

From *Thao Hung Thao Cheuang* by Doungdeuane (Viravongs) Bounyavong, Vientiane. Retold by Wajuppa Tossa.

This rather confusing story is believed to record historical events and is included here because of its importance to Lao tradition.

*T*hao Hung was a son of Khun Chomtham, ruler of Suantan or Nakhong Kingdom (now Chiangrai, Thailand). When he was three years old, the Phangdam tribe presented him with a sword and a couple of silver gongs, and later on he was offered a white elephant named Xangpheuakphankham. Khun Chomtham died when Thao Hung was in his teens. His mother, together with the people of Suantan Kingdom, crowned Thao Hung's elder brother, Thao Cheuang, as the ruler of Muang Suantan, and Thao Hung was his viceroy. Thao Hung trained his elephant in the arts of warfare, and sometimes he rode it to faraway places. One day he met Nang Ngom, daughter of Nang Meng, who was a ruling princess of the Kingdom of Xieng Kheua (Nang Meng was Thao Hung's aunt). Thao Hung fell in love with Nang Ngom, so he requested his elders to ask for her hand in marriage from her mother. Nang Meng demanded too much bride price for Thao Hung to afford. Thao Hung therefore secretly entered his lover's room to consummate their love.

At that time there was a Vietnamese prince from Muang Khamwang named Einka; he was the nephew of Thao Kua, ruler of Muang Pakan (the city now called Xieng Khouang). After his father's death, Einka became ruler of Muang Khamwang. At that time, he was not yet married, and he wanted to marry a beautiful girl. Hearing of one named Nang Oua, daughter of Khunjum, king of Muang Ngoenyang (the city now known as Chiang Saen in Thailand), he sent an envoy to ask her hand in marriage, but Khunjum did not agree. Moreover, Khunjum told the envoy that he would give Nang Oua to his own nephew, Thao Hung. (Khunjum was the elder brother of Thao Hung's dead father, Khun Chomtham.)

On receiving this report from his envoy, Einka hastened to inform his uncle, King Thao Kua, at Muang Pakan. The latter was so angry that he sent an envoy to King Khunjum threatening that, if he did not agree to let his daughter marry Einka, his kingdom would be in jeopardy. Khunjum, hearing this, was also angered, and immediately told the envoy:

Since I have ruled Ngoenyang,
No-one, but you, dared to utter arrogant words.
He who marries my daughter must be of her race;
No-one else has the right to speak thus.

When these insults were reported to King Thao Kua and his nephew, Einka, they were infuriated, and they led their armies to attack Muang Ngoenyang. Eleven of Einka's commanders took part in this war, including Hunbang and others.

While they were marching toward Ngoenyang, King Thao Kua told Naymat to ask Samma-heng, chief of the Phu Thum tribe, for directions and for help. Thao Kua also asked Aiyhad, chief of the Pha Lod tribe, for help. Samma-heng and Aiyhad then were told to lead his troops ahead. However, Samma-heng and Aiyhad, who were allies of King Khunjum, decided to inform Khunjum about the attack so that he could be ready for it. Khunjum, hearing of his enemies' plot, prepared to defend his kingdom.

Khunjum's troops could not resist Einka's army, so they withdrew into the town. Khunjum then sent a message to his nephew Thao Hung, asking for help. The latter set off with his army to aid his uncle. His generals were Aiykhuang, Einkhon, Hengphay, Khunkhan, Khonxay, and Chason. At the same time, Nang Ngom, Thao Hung's lover from Xiengkheua, commanded a troop of twenty elephants and many important generals to fight along side Thao Hung

Arriving in Ngoenyang, Thao Hung's troops, together with Princess Nang Ngom and her troops, attacked Einka's soldiers, who were hiding in the surrounding area. The latter fled in disorder and split into small groups. In the course of the fighting Thao Kua, prince of Pakan, was killed on the battlefield, while Einka was captured by Khun-yia, Princess Nang Ngom's general. Thao Kua's commanders were also killed. The rest of Einka's troops, 30,000 in number, were captured. But Hunbang managed to escape.

In this war, Thao Hung lost 3,000 men. When the war was over Thao Hung, with the three armies from Suantan, Xiangkheua, and Ngoenyang, had driven their enemy up to the frontier. Thao Hung's army returned home in the fifth month with the ladies Nang Oua, daughter of King Khunjum, and Nang Amkha, accompanying him as far as the land called Xiangkhuan. Nang Oua rode an elephant named Phang-hoen-pakhuemad, while Nang Amkha rode an elephant named Inkong. From there, Thao Hung led his army to Tha-yong Phalod, where he found a number of elephants and horses that had belonged to Einka's general, Hunbang. But Hunbang escaped. Then Thao Hung's army went to Phu Thum, where the Phangdam tribe lived. After Phu Thum, they arrived at Muang Pakan on the same day.

The following morning, Thao Hung and his army attacked Xiangban. According to a local chronicle, Xiangban had a population of 500,000 and 1,000 elephants. Its borders were Sithom in Khen (Khmer) and Ho (Lao Nongsae). Xiangban was seized that morning. Kaewphoeng, Thao Daed, and Maenhuang were captured. Kaewhuak jumped off the elephant's back and fled to Muang Pakan to tell Thao Kua's wife to defend the city. Thao Kua's wife rode out on an elephant leading an army to fight against Thao Hung, until she was killed in the battle. After Thao Hung seized Muang Pakan, he appointed his noblemen and ministers to administer fourteen sections of Xiangkuan region and to oversee the tribute collection:

1. Khun-yia ruled the large rice field, and was in charge of elephant tribute.

2. Einkhon ruled Xiang Ban rice field, a prosperous trade center.

3. Khonxay ruled Kongthun rice field, where they levied more agricultural produce.

4. Patcim (the western) rice field, which was the border of Phalod region, was apportioned to Nang Meng.

5. Nakham rice field, which formerly belonged to the land of Kaewkam, was apportioned to Xaylue.

6. The plain rice field of Pha Tham was apportioned to Einphay.

7. The rice field of Maenluean was apportioned to Nanoy.

8. The rice field of Maenfay was under the administration of Ngoenyang.

9. The abundant rice field of Xiang Khuan, with its betel leaf, areca nut, and coconut plants, were apportioned to Nang Oua.

10. The rice field of Dong Chan was apportioned to Nang Amkha.

11. The rice field of Khamwang was apportioned to Aiy-keuan

12. The rice field of Kaew Heuak, in the eastern sector at the Chinese border, was kept as a tributary state.

13. The rice field on the Bang Bin River bank was apportioned to Uncle Phouang.

14. The plain rice field outside of the city was apportioned to Chason.

Thao Hung nominated Thao Khuang ruler of Muang Pakan. After he finished his duties, he led his army back to Ngoenyang via Xiangban. After ten days, he arrived home. Upon his arrival, he asked Nang Chom, his mother, to be the ruler of Xiangkhuan, which was the border city of Muang Pakan. Thao Hung ruled Ngoenyang for seventeen years. Nang Ngom bore him a son named Thao Khamhung. While he was ruling Ngoenyang, the following foreign guests brought him tribute:

1. Ho Nhay (Grand Ho) of Nongsae

2. Phya Fa-huan of Tumwang

3. Ruler of a Chinese Kingdom

4. Rulers of Muang Phakho, Muang Nan, and Muang Chawa

5. Rulers of Muang Phayi, as well as Khmer and Lue

Later on Hunbang, commander-in-chief of Thao Einka, who had fled and taken refuge with Phya Fa-huan of the court of Tumwang, led guerrillas to attack Pakan territory. Aiykhuang, the ruler of Pakan, reported this to Thao Hung, who immediately sent troops to Tumwang to subjugate Hunbang. There, Thao Hung's envoy, Khun Khon, negotiated with

Phya Fa-huan over the matter of surrendering Hunbang and Thao Hing, but Phya Fa-huan refused to do so, saying that both men had requested refuge in his court. When the negotiation failed, Thao Hung decided to attack Tumwang.

Phya Fa-huan was not strong enough to resist the attack, so he sent Maensom to submit to Thao Hung, but the latter did not accept this protocol, not trusting the enemy. He decided to overthrow Tumwang. Phya Fa-huan therefore sent two of his soldiers to seek help from Thaen Lo of the Kingdom of Kalong. The distance between Tumwang and Kalong was fifteen days' journey by oxcart. Upon arrival, Thaen Lo led his army to fight a bloody battle against Thao Hung and his troops. Most of Thao Hung's generals were killed, so he withdrew to Muang Pakan, sending a message to tell Aiycheuang and Khunjum (his father-in-law) to send reinforcements. The fighting was so fierce that Nay Phouang, one of Thao Hung's generals, feared that if they fought to the last man, it would result in genocide. He therefore asked permission to send away his mother, Nang Chomsom, and the children, among whom were Thao Khamkheuang and Thao Khamhung, sons of Thao Hung to Ngoenyang, while Thao Hung himself fought on until he was killed on the battlefield.

The local chronicle further states that, after his death, Thao Hung's spirit became commander-in-chief of the ghost army. He led these troops to attack the Thaen Kingdom through Muang Khakhiow. Einkhon, his most important general, had gone to ask Tai Eing the way to Muang Fa (Thaen's city in heaven). It was also said they had to go by monkeys' ladder, by which they reached Linkham River toward Muang Lianphan, which was Thaen's city. After conquering Muangphan, Thao Hung led his ghost troops toward the luminescent land of Indra. At Muang Kongthun, Thaen Lom, the city ruler there, paid him homage. At Muang Kamma, Thaen Nguang paid homage to Thao Hung. After that he passed other cities of Thaen, and they all came to pay homage to him. These Thaen city rulers included Thaenthao, Thaenmeng, Thaenkokay, Thaen-thuang, Thaenfeuang, Thaenmok, Thaenlee, Thaenlom, and Thaensong.

Meanwhile, Thao Cheuang (Thao Hung's elder brother), Khunjum, Thao Khamheuang, and Thao Khamhung led the troops from Ngoenyang to attack Phya Fa-huan again. Finally, Phya Fa-huan was killed and the troops from Ngoenyang occupied Tumwang.

And the story ends at this point.

PART 13

Lao Food, Crafts, and Games

LAO CRAFTS

Arts and crafts are related to the Lao people's way of life and economic purposes. Each of the different groups of Lao people has passed on its arts and crafts from the older generation of grandparents to succeeding generations. Each group has its own identity in arts and crafts, but they are similar in many ways. Lao arts and crafts include basket weaving, pottery, and blacksmithing. The products of these arts and crafts are for their own use in the family and for exchange for other arts and crafts. They also produce ornaments from silver and gold.

Lao women are well-known for their excellent arts and crafts. They create these from scratch, beginning by planting cotton and mulberry, raising silk worms on the mulberry leaves, spinning and spooling the cotton and silk threads, dying, weaving, and embroidering. In almost every house there are looms and other weaving tools for making cloth to make clothes for the entire family. The daughters will learn these arts and crafts to pass on to their children.

Children observe adults doing all these arts and crafts and try to create their own "artworks," which become their toys and playthings. This section describes are a few of these arts and crafts.

Baisii

Adults use banana leaves to make trays of flowers to present to the temple for worship or to be part of a *baisii* ceremony. The *baisii* tray is made from banana leaves. Banana leaves are cut into 4-by-5-inch rectangular pieces. The women roll each piece of banana leaf into a pyramid shape or funnel. After they have enough, they string 5 to 15 funnels together to make a spike. Strips of banana leaf are used to bind the funnels together. Five to nine spikes are used to surround a cone made of a bigger piece of banana leaf, which is set in the center of a tray. Then flowers are placed at the end of each pointed spike and arranged around the tray.

In making the *baisii* some pieces may be tossed aside as unusable or unneeded. The children collect these thrown away pieces and put them together to make their own crafts. They might make a porcupine or a bird of paradise flower as toys. Or the children may search for young and flexible leaves 2 or 3 inches long and imitate what the adults are doing. They roll each leaf into a cone with a pointed tip, then use toothpicks to string them together to make a spike. After they get 3 spikes, they put them together into any shape they can imagine, which could be a porcupine or a bird of paradise flower. Sometimes they use scraps of paper in place of the leaves and follow the same steps, using glue or double-sided tape to fasten the pieces together.

Bird of paradise flower and porcupine made from paper cones

Loy Kathong Float

Adults use banana leaves to make floats for a festival called *Loy Kathong* on the full moon night of the twelfth lunar month. This falls sometime between the end of October and the beginning of December. Children may try their hands at making *Loy Kathong* floats as well.

You can make a small *Loy Kathong* float. If you make this out of leaves, you can float it on a stream. Or you can make it out of paper and use it as a little basket on your desk.

1. Use banana leaves or colored paper. You need 9 to 15 square or rectangular pieces of leaf or colored paper, 3 by 3 or 3 by 4 inches in size. Some sizable leaves, such as lilac leaves, could be used in place of banana leaves or paper.

2. Form 8 petals by rolling each piece of paper or each leaf into a pointed cone for the outer layer of the float.

3. Prepare a circular piece of cardboard 2 or 3 inches in diameter for the base if you are making a paper basket. To make a floatable *Loy Kathong,* use a ½-inch-thick circular piece cut from the middle of an apple for the base of the float. In Laos this base would be made of a slice from a banana tree trunk.

4. Glue the petals around the edge of the circular paper base. If you are making your *Loy Kathong* of leaves, fasten each of the leaf petals around the apple base with half of a toothpick.

5. Make smaller petals from paper squares 1½ inches long for the inner layer of the basket or float.

6. Arrange the smaller petals inside the outer layer of the leaf petals and fasten them with glue (paper basket) or toothpicks (leaf basket).

7. Place small flowers in the float and at the tip of each of the petals.

On *Loy Kathong* night these little baskets made of banana leaf are floated in a pond or river. If yours is made of leaves, you can float it in a stream.

Rolled leaves for the *Kathong*

Apple slice *Kathong*

Floating *Kathong*

If you have made yours of paper, use it as a small basket for paper clips or other small articles.

Cones to make basket

Paper cone basket

Kong Khaen Leaf Bracelet

A simple bracelet can be made of a coconut leaf or strips of a banana leaf. If you cannot find large enough leaves, you can make this of paper.

1. Prepare a strip of paper 3 times as long as your wrist measures around. The strip should be around ½-inch wide.

2. Cut the strip down the middle, but not all the way. Leave ½ inch of uncut strip at the end so as to have one piece of strip with two legs.

3. Fold one strip down across the other. Press it flat. Then fold the other strip over this one. Press it flat. Do this until the end of the paper. Glue the two ends of the strip together to make a circle.

See the illustrations for how the bracelet is made and what it will look like.

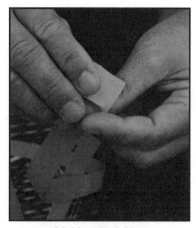

Making the folds

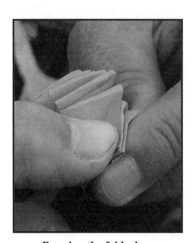

Pressing the folds down

Gluing the ends together

LAO FOOD

Lao people like to eat simple food because they have to work hard in the fields. They have little time to make elaborate dishes. The main staple is sticky rice, eaten at every meal. Sticky rice requires soaking for at least two to four hours before steaming it in a bamboo basket that fits over a bubbling cooking pot. It takes about fifteen to thirty minutes to cook, depending on the amount of soaked rice and the temperature used. If the heat is high and there is not much rice, it could take only fifteen to twenty minutes to cook.

After the rice is cooked, it is put in a sticky rice box. It is eaten by rolling small balls of rice together in the right hand. Nowadays, when time is short, sticky rice may be cooked in an electric cooking pot with a little less water than used when cooking other kinds of rice. But sticky rice cooked this way cannot be eaten properly by rolling it in the hand.

Rice goes with many dishes. Lao methods of cooking include roasting, steaming, simple baking, and mixing. Following are a few examples of Lao food that can be cooked easily.

1. Roast fish, chicken, or any kind of meat: Clean the fish or the meat, sprinkle salt on it, put it between two bamboo sticks, and roast it over a flame. Serve with rice.

2. *Laab*, or *koi*—spicy minced meat (chicken, pork, beef, fish, shrimp, or lamb) salad: *Laab* and *koi* have similar ingredients and method of cooking. The only differences between the two are that (1) the *laab* can be juicier and *koi* must be quite dry, and (2) *laab* requires minced meat and *koi* requires thin slices of meat.

   Laab is minced meat of some kind (chicken, fish, beef, shrimp) mixed with salted fish sauce, salt, chili pepper, sliced green onions, finely sliced cilantro, finely chopped blue ginger, lime juice, and ground roasted rice. If all of these ingredients are not available, both *laab* and *koi* can be prepared without them. The most important ingredients are the meat, onions, salted fish sauce (may be replaced with soy sauce), and lime juice.

Laab paa Salmon (Salmon *Laab*)

Ingredients:

- ½ lb. cooked salmon
- ½ tsp salt
- 1 tbsp green onions
- 1 tbsp cilantro
- 2 tbsp fish sauce (or soy sauce)
- 1 tbsp lime juice

Directions:

1. Chop the salmon.
2. Stir in the salt, green onions, and cilantro.
3. Add the fish sauce and lime juice.
4. Mix everything together.
5. Eat with rice.

Serves two.

Ingredients for *laab*

***Laab* ready to serve**

Chopped and cooked ingredients

Tam maak hung or *yam maak hung* (Green Papaya Salad)

Note: This is a popular Lao dish. Since green papaya may be difficult for readers to find, we have given a version using carrots. But make it with green papaya if you can!

The word *tam* refers to the method of pounding things with a mortar and pestle; the word *yam* refers to the mixing of things in a bowl or other container. Carrot, green apple, or cabbage could be used to replace the green papaya.

Ingredients:

3 carrots, peeled (or 1 small green papaya)
1 medium tomato, chopped
1 small clove garlic
1 small chili pepper (chopped very fine or pounded in a mortar)
2 tbsp fish sauce or soy sauce
1 tbsp sugar or honey
1 tbsp lime or lemon juice

Directions:

1. Grate the carrots.
2. Mix in the chili pepper, fish sauce, and sugar or honey.
3. Add the lime or lemon juice.
4. Mix all ingredients thoroughly.
5. Taste and add more salt, soy sauce, and lime or lemon juice as needed. For those who do not like hot spicy food, the chili pepper may be left out.

Serves two.

Tam maak hung ingredients

Chopped *Tam maak hung* ingredients

Tam maak hung served on lettuce leaves

Phan Phak (Fresh Vegetable Spring Rolls) and Peanut Sauce

Ingredients:

1 cup bean sprouts

½ lb. shrimp, chicken, beef, pork, or fish

1 tbsp olive oil

½ cup onion, chopped

1 tsp salt

8 large lettuce leaves

4 tbsp green onions, chopped

4 tbsp cilantro

4 tbsp basil leaves

4 tbsp fresh mint leaves

Directions:

1. Steam the bean sprouts in a microwave for 1 minute.

2. Sauté the shrimp in the olive oil with the onion and salt for 5–10 minutes or cook for 2 minutes in a microwave.

3. Arrange the sprouts, shrimp, lettuce, green onions, cilantro, basil, and mint on a large plate in little piles (or in separate small bowls).

4. Put a teaspoon of each ingredient onto a lettuce leaf and roll it up. Dip this roll in peanut sauce and eat.

Makes 8 rolls.

Peanut sauce

Ingredients:

1 tbsp salt

½ cup sugar

½ cup boiling water

½ cup finely chopped peanuts

1 tsp finely chopped garlic

2 tbsp lime or lemon juice

diced or ground chili pepper to taste

Directions:

1. Combine the salt, sugar, and boiling water. Stir until salt and sugar are dissolved.
2. Add the peanuts, garlic, juice, and pepper.
3. Stir again.

Note: To make the sauce thicker, boil the water, sugar, and salt over a low fire for 5–7 minutes before adding the other ingredients.

Phan Phak ingredients

Chopped and cooked *Phan Phak* ingredients

Prepared rolls with dipping sauce

Dipping the rolls

CHILDREN'S GAMES

Many Lao children's games originally were created by adolescent boys and girls. They made up various games as courting opportunities. They played these games in their free time, during ceremonies, when people got together, or at festivals. One of these games is called *mak li* (hide and seek). The children watching the teenagers playing such games remembered and imitated them. Over time these became children's games, and the children played them regardless of the occasion. Here are a few games that children adapted to play.

Game 1: Throwing a Cloth-ball (*Maak Yon Ao Laeng—throwing for a servant*)

Needed:
- A piece of cloth rolled and tied tightly into a ball
- A line drawn between the two sides

Players:
- There is no limit to the number of players.
- Players are divided into 2 sides of equal numbers.

Time limit:
- The two sides agree on the time limit: 5, 10, 15, or 20 minutes.

Object of the game:
- To have the most players at the end of the time limit.
- The game is over when the time is up or when any side has only 1 player left.

How to play:

- Players stand in 2 straight lines facing each other.
- Draw a line down the middle. The 2 sides should be about 20 to 30 feet apart.
- Any side can begin the game by throwing the cloth-ball to the opposite side. The opposite side must try to catch the ball and throw it back to the first side. If the ball is not caught and is dropped by any side, that side will have to send 1 player to the other side. The game continues until the time is up or one side has only 1 player left. The side with more players is the winner.

Game 2: Snake Biting Its Tail *(Maak Ngu Gin Hang)*

Players:

- 10–20 players (more if desired)
- One person to be the referee.

Object of the game:

- The head of the snake must try to catch the last player in the line.
- Once that person is caught, the game is over. The game begins with the person caught playing the head of the snake. The game is also over if any player loses grip of the waist of the person in front.

How to play:

- The players stand in a straight line facing one direction. Each player holds onto the waist of the player in front. The first player at the head of the line plays the head of the snake; the rest of the players form the tail.
- When the referee says "1, 2, 3, go," the head tries to go to the tail, and the rest of the players must try to prevent this by swaying away from the direction that the head is going, without breaking the line.
- When the time is up and the head still has not caught the tail, the game begins again. If the head catches the tail, the game is over and may start again, with the person who was caught now playing the part of the head.

Game 3: The Turtle Eggs (*Maak Khai Tao*)

Needed:

- 10–20 small rocks or small balls to be used as "turtle eggs"
- a circular line of about 2 feet in diameter around the mother turtle and the eggs

Players:

- 5–10 players

Time limit:

- 5–10 minutes

Object of the game:

- The mother turtle must guard all the turtle eggs during the time limit. The other players try to take as many eggs as possible without being touched by the mother turtle.

How to play:

- Set the eggs in the center of a circle with the mother turtle inside the circle. The mother turtle must not go outside of the circle, and the other players must try to get the eggs without being touched by the mother turtle.
- Whoever is touched by the mother turtle becomes the mother turtle, and the previous mother turtle becomes one of the players.
- When the time is up, if nobody has been touched and no egg has been taken, the player who is the mother turtle continues being the mother turtle in a new game.

Game 4: Shooting the Targets (*Maak Baa*)

Note: Maak baa is a round, flat, hard seed from a vine. It's dark brown and very smooth and shiny, about ½ inch thick and 2–3 inches in diameter. Any round throat lozenge tin can or round candy tin can of 2–3 inches in diameter or an empty roll of tape of 2–3 inches in diameter could be used. The *maak baa* is used in two ways, as the hitter and as targets.

Needed:

- Each side has 1 hitter and a number of targets (e.g., 2–4 targets for each hitter). If there are 5 players and each uses 3 targets, the total targets would be 15.

Players:

- Players are divided into two sides, with 4–5 players on each side

Object of the game:

- Each side tries to knock down as many targets as possible. When all the targets are knocked down, the game is over. A knocked down target belongs to the shooter. The side with more targets is the winner.

How to shoot or throw:

There are various ways of shooting the hitter:

1. Put the hitter flat on the ground and use two index fingers to shoot it.
2. Place the hitter on one knee and use two index fingers to shoot it.
3. Simply toss or throw the hitter with one hand.

The other side may challenge the player to throw or shoot in any style, such as carrying the hitter between the toes and hopping on one foot to come and hit the target, or throwing the hitter backward, or throwing or tossing it blindfolded. If it can be done, the player may get more than one target as a reward.

How to play:

- Set the targets up on the side in 1 straight line. Draw the beginning line about 20 feet away from the line of targets.
- Once the targets for each player have been set up in one straight line, the leader of each side will stand at the beginning line. After counting 1, 2, 3, the leader will roll the hitter toward the target line. When the hitter falls or stops, it must not be moved because it becomes the shooting spot for the two sides.
- The owner of the hitter that stops nearest to the line of the targets will begin the game by throwing the hitter at one of the targets to knock it down. If it is knocked down, this side will have another turn.
- The next player will wait until the hitter stops rolling and will go to shoot the target from that spot.

- If the hitter does not knock down any of the targets, the leader of the other side will have a turn to try to knock down one of the targets. The leader will shoot from the spot at which his or her hitter stopped in the opening roll of the two leaders.
- The game continues until all the targets are knocked down. The side that knocks down the most targets is the winner.

NOTES ON TALE SOURCES
AND MOTIFS

In the notes I give references to folktale motif-indexes that have included these stories. The sources I refer to are listed here. You may consult these indexes as well as the sources cited in the tale notes to find more variants of the stories shared here.

Aarne, Antti, and Stith Thompson. *The Types of the Folktale.* Helsinki: Folklore Fellows Communication, 1961.

MacDonald, Margaret Read. *The Storyteller's Sourcebook: A Subject, Title, and Motif-Index to Folklore Collections for Children.* 1st ed. Detroit: Neal-Schuman/Gale Research, 1982.

MacDonald, Margaret Read, and Brian W. Sturm. *The Storyteller's Sourcebook: A Subject, Title, and Motif-Index to Folklore Collections for Children: 1983-1999.* Farmington Hills, MI: Gale Group, 2000.

Thompson, Stith. *Motif-Index of Folk-Literature.* 6 vols. Bloomington: Indiana University Press, 1966.

Part 2: Buddhist *Jātaka* and Moral Tales

Phra Wetsandon Xadouk. Retold by Kongdeuane Nettavong, Vientiane, Laos. Translated by Wajuppa Tossa. This story is well known to all Lao Buddhists. For another retelling, see "Sacred White Elephants and a Youth's Generous Ways: The Story of Vetsandon," in *Encircled Kingdom: Legends and Folktales of Laos* (Thousand Oaks, CA: Burn, Hart, 1979). For more information on the story of Prince Vessantara (Phra Wetsandon) and the use of the classic epic in modern Thai literature and another version of the story, please go to the following sites: http://www.seasite.niu.edu/Tha/Literature/sridaouruang/matsii/matsii2.htm and http://www.seasite.niu.edu/lao/JatakaTales. *H1552 Test of generosity.*

The Turtle and the Swans. Told by Phra Inta Kaweewong, Wat Sa-ahdsomboon, Roi-et Province, Thailand. Collected and retold in English by Wajuppa Tossa. *J2357 Tor-*

---

toise speaks and loses his hold on the stick. He is being carried through the air by a bird. MacDonald gives variants from India, Somalia, Bemba, China, Ceylon, Russia, Nicaragua, and Haiti. MacDonald & Sturm give variants from China, France, India, and Mexico. *K1041 Borrowed feathers.* Dupe lets himself be carried aloft by bird and dropped. MacDonald & Sturm give variants from Mexico, Khoikhoi, Cherokee, and other Native American. MacDonald gives variants from The Ukraine; Berber; Chuckchee; Swahili; Hausa; African American; Russia; East Africa; Liberia; West Indies; Haiti; Eskimo; Nicaragua. *J657.2 Tortoise lets self be carried by eagle.*

A Flying Lesson. Told by Phra Sunantha Theerapanyo Phikkhu. Collected and retold in English by Wajuppa Tossa. *K1041 Borrowed feathers.* See tale note for "The Turtle and the Swans," above.

The Three Friends. Adapted from versions by Phra Inta Kaweewong, Wat Sa-ahdsomboon, Roi-et Province, Thailand, and Mantchanok Thongkanok, Muang Samsip School, Ubon Ratchathani, Thailand. Collected and retold in English by Wajuppa Tossa. *B841.1 Animals debate as to which is the elder.* Stith Thompson cites variants from India, Korea, Japan, Africa (Benga, Fang). MacDonald gives stories on this theme from Korea, Tibet, India, China, Haiti, Wales, and Africa (Ashanti).

The Golden Swan. Told by Phra Soubandit Duangwongsa, Wat Saphanthongnue, Vientiane, Laos. Collected and retold in English by Wajuppa Tossa. *D876 Magic Treasure Animal Killed.* The most commonly known tale based on this motif is the Aesop fable, "The goose that laid the golden egg." Stith Thompson cites also tales from India (Panchatantra), Japan, Indonesia, and a Native American tale. This unusual tale contains also *D161.1 Transformation: Man to swan. W151 Greed.*

The Magic White Swan. Told by Sivilay Sopha, Vientiane, Laos. Retold in English by Wajuppa Tossa. *B546.2 Helpful Swan. W151 Greed. J2415 Foolish imitation of lucky man.* Tales of the kind and unkind person are told throughout the world. This particular tale, in which the man is carried by a swan, is unique from most others. Stith Thompson cites a tale from India that may be related to this story. *B542.2.1 Transportation to fairyland on griffin's back.*

Part 3: Tales of Xiang Miang and Other Tricksters

The most famous Lao trickster is the novice monk Xiang Miang. He is known in Thailand as Sri Thanonchai, and his adventures there are believed to date from the Ayutthaya period (A.D. 1350–1767). Wat Pathum Wanarum in Bangkok, built by King Mongkut in 1857, features murals depicting the adventures of Sri Thanonchai. For more Xiang Miang tales, see "Xieng Mieng Stories," in *Encircled Kingdom: Legends and Folktale of Laos* by Jewell Reinhard Coburn (Thousand Oaks, CA: Burn, Hart, 1979), pp. 37–40.

The Birth of Xiang Miang. Told by Jinda Duangjai, Kamalasai, Kalasin, Thailand. Collected and retold in English by Wajuppa Tossa. Mr. Duangjai set this story down from some palm leaf manuscripts he was able to examine. *Ruam Nithan Isan [A collection of Northeast Thai Folktales]* by Jinda Duangjai (Khonkaen: Klang Nanatham, 1962). *D1812.3.3.8 Dream by a (pregnant) woman about fate of her unborn child.* In this tale Xiang Miang becomes a novice monk for the king's funeral. This is a usual thing for a devout son to do for his father. The young man will shave his head and don the robes of a monk and behave as a monk during the funeral ceremonies. In the case of Xiang Miang, he chose to remain a monk for some time. Stith Thompson cites a tale from India using a similar double-meaning ploy. *K232.1 By using verse with double-meaning man appropriates borrowed goods.*

Xiang Miang Outwits the King. Retold by Wajuppa Tossa. This tale is also found in *Thai Tales: Folktales of Thailand* by Supaporn Vathanaprida (Libraries Unlimited, 1994), pp. 17–18, told of Sri Thanonchai (the Thai equivalent of Xiang Miang). And it may be found in *The Serpent Prince: Folktales of Northeastern Thailand* by Kermit Krueger (New York: World, 1969), pp 144–50, as "Sieng-mieng, the Minister." A similar tale appears in *Zen Flesh, Zen Bones* by Paul Rep (Garden City, NY: Doubleday, 1961), pp. 8–9. In this latter, Japanese tale, Bankei tricks a Nichiren priest into obeying him. MacDonald & Sturm assign this motif *K93. Bet won by deception.*

Xiang Miang Finds the Best Food for the King. Told by Jinda Duangjai, Kamalasai, Kalasin, Thailand. Collected and retold in English by Wajuppa Tossa. Stith Thompson gives us *J1606 Two monks renew their appetites.* Entertained by a lord, they say they are going to certain waters to recover their appetites. They are taken to a chamber and locked in for a day. They recover their appetites without further journeying. He cites German and Italian versions, including one from Boccaccio. *J1606.1 Hungry man eats intestines of fish next morning after refusing to do so the evening before.* One variant, from India. In a slightly different tale, the Thai Sri Thanonchai offers to cook for the king the world's most tasty and most unsavory dishes. He brings tongue for both. Tongue sings. Tongue curses.

Xiang Miang and the Snail. Told by Kunthari Saichua, grade one, Anuban Ubon Ratchathani School, Ubon Ratchathani, Thailand. Collected and retold in English by Wajuppa Tossa. *K11.1 Race won by deception, relative helpers.* MacDonald cites variants in which snail wins from Indonesia and Liberia.

Xiang Miang Sees the King's Face. English translation by Wajuppa Tossa, from a secondary student's version in an English-language storytelling camp in Kosumwitthayasan School, Kosumphisai, Mahasarakham, Thailand. This tale is reminiscent of *F511.2.2 Person with ass's (horse's ears)*. *Variants of that tale, though, lack the clever way to peek a look motif. C310 Tabu: looking at certain person or thing.*

Xiang Miang Tricks the King. Told by Jinda Duangjai, Kamalasai, Kalasin, Thailand. Retold in English by Wajuppa Tossa. For a similar tale, see "Sri Thanonchai and the King," in *Thai Tales: Folktales of Thailand* by Supaporn Vathanaprida (Libraries Unlimited, 1994), pp. 17–18.

The Novice and the Abbot. Told by Suched Somsa, a storytelling student at Mahasarakham University, Mahasarakham, Thailand. Collected and retold in English by Wajuppa Tossa. *K1044 Dupe induced to eat filth (dung).* This seems to occur in many cultures. Stith Thompson cites this motif from Ireland, Italy, Indonesia, The Marquesas, Hawaii, and West Indies.

The Abbot and the Novice Carry Salt. Told by a storytelling student at Mahasarakham University, Mahasarakham, Thailand. Collected and retold in English by Wajuppa Tossa. Folktales centering on salt's melting quality occur in several cultures. *J1612 The lazy ass repaid in kind. Loaded with salt, he falls down in the river and lightens his burden.* This is an Aesop fable. Type 211 gives Flemish, Hungarian, and West Indian versions of this. *K25.2 Contest in flying with load. One animal chooses cotton, the other, seeing that a rain is coming, chooses salt and wins.*

Part 4: Tales of Fools

The Day Dreamer. From "Building Castle in the Air," by Samrit Buasisavath, in *The Great Gourd of Heaven: A Selection of the Folk-tales and Stories of Laos.* Collected by Roisin O Boyle and Thavisack Phanmathanh (Vientiane: Vannasin Magazine, The Ministry of Information and Culture, 1992), pp. 47–51. Retold in English by Wajuppa Tossa. *J2060 Absurd plans. Air-castles. Type 1430. Air-castle: basket of glassware to be sold. In his excitement he breaks the glassware.*

The Crescent Moon Comb. Told by Phatcharaphorn Dongruangsi, grade 11, Thetoon Village, Thailand, who heard the story from her grandmother. Collected and retold in English by Wajuppa Tossa. *J1795 Image in mirror mistaken.* MacDonald cites versions of this tale from Japan, Korea, China, and Wales. She has also heard a Southern Indiana variant of this told as a foolish Kentuckian joke. MacDonald & Sturm cite variants from China, Korea, England, and the American Southwest.

The Foolish Family. As told by ninth grader Khambao Thaenna, Mahasarakham, Thailand. Collected and retold in English by Wajuppa Tossa. *J2063 Distress over imagined troubles of unborn child.* Stith Thompson cites the German tale of Clever Else, who went to the cellar to get wine and began weeping over a hatchet that might fall and kill the son she might have one day. Her parents join her and the suitor leaves in disgust.

Part 5: Animal Tales

Why Owl Has a Flat Head and Yellow Eyes. Told by Sivilay Sopha, Vientiane, Laos. Retold in English by Wajuppa Tossa. Sivilay has also written this tale in picture book format. In a tale contributed by Bounyok Saensounthone of Vientiane, Laos, the story is told of a cicada whose call is:

> *Lii lae lii lae*
> *Caa*
> *Khwaung hae*
> *Sai hua nok khao*
>
> *Lii lae lii lae*
> *I will dare*
> *Cast a net*
> *Over the head of that owl.*

This frightened owl so that he said "*hok sak hok sak*" (I will throw a lance. I will throw a lance). This frightened deer, who kicked sesame seeds, which blinded pheasant, who scratched ant's nest, who bit snake's naval, who bit gourd's vine, which fell on the head of baby chameleon. Chameleon went to the lion, King of the Jungle, for justice. The chain is traced back to Cicada. He is forced to pay tribute, but has nothing to pay with, so his insides are taken as payment. Hence Cicada has a hollow body today. *Z49.6 Trial among the animals.* The tale appears with a variety of difference animals in the chain, but always an animal goes to ask judgment for damage done, usually to its children. Stith Thompson cites variants from India, Indonesia, Malaya, and the Philippines. In another motif, *Z43.1 Fly frightens snake, snake frightens rat, rat frightens monkeys, etc.* Thompson gives African variants (Fang, Duala, Swahili, and from the Cameroon). MacDonald gives variants from the Philippines (Pampangan), Nigeria (Ekoi), West Indies, China, Assam, Indonesia, Burma, and India.

Maeng Nguan, the Singing Cricket. Told by Bounyok Saensunthone, Vientiane, Laos. Collected and retold in English by Wajuppa Tossa. Bounyok used to be a teacher of monks in Vientiane. He works now with palm leaf manuscript preservation. Recorded by Wajuppa Tossa. Translated and retold by Wajuppa Tossa. Some of the tales she recorded in more than one telling from Bounyok. *A2426.3.4 Cricket's chirp. A2411.5.6*

Color of chameleon. A2411.5.2 Color of frog. You may hear Maha Bounyok Sainsounthone telling this story in Lao at http://www.seasite.niu.edu/lao/.

Why Dog Lifts His Leg. Told by Bounyok Saensounthone, Vientiane, Laos. Collected and retold in English by Wajuppa Tossa. *A2473.1 Why dog lifts his leg.* Stith Thompson gives a tale from Japan. MacDonald cites a Vietnamese version in which the Buddha gives dog a lotus blossom as a hind leg, which he must not soil. You may hear Maha Bounyok Saensounthone telling this story in Lao at http://www.seasite.niu.edu/lao/.

The Tiger's Stripes. Told by Phra Sunantha Theeraphanyo, Vientiane, Laos. Collected and retold in English by Wajuppa Tossa. The story appears also in *Thai Tales: Folktales of Thailand* by Supaporn Vathanaprida (Libraries Unlimited, 1994), pp. 29–30. She gives sources from Surin and Chiangmai. This is related to *Motif K341.8.1 Trickster pretends to ride home for tools to perform tricks.* MacDonald cites variants from Russia (Tatar), Scandinavia, Turkey, Vietnam, and Native American. A Thai variant (Surin-Sisaket) is found in *Thai Tales: Folktales of Thailand* by Supaporn Vathanaprida (Libraries Unlimited, 1994), pp. 29–30. This tale is identical except that the farmer simply beats the Tiger, so it lacks the burnt rice straw and stripes element. *A2413.4 Stripes of tiger. Thompson gives tales from India and China showing why tiger has stripes.*

Why Pythons Are Not Poisonous. Told by Bounyok Saensounthone, Vientiane, Laos. Collected and retold in English by Wajuppa Tossa. *A 2532.1 Why snakes are venomous. A2532 Why animals are venomous.* Other cultures also have tales relating why certain snakes are not venomous. For *A2531.1 Why water serpents are not venomous,* Stith Thompson cites tales from India, Africa (Congo), and Native American (Pueblo). You may hear Maha Bounyok Saensounthone telling this tale in Lao at http://www.seasite.niu.edu/lao/.

The Baldheaded Lesser Adjutant Stork, Nok Kaxoum Hou Laan. Told by Bounyok Saensounthone, Vientiane, Laos. Collected and retold in English by Wajuppa Tossa. *Z49.6 Trial among the animals.* See discussion of this motif under "Why Owl Has a Flat Head and Yellow Eyes" above. *A2317 Why certain animals are bare of covering.* Stith Thompson gives tales here explaining why buzzard, crow, raven, magpie, and vulture are bald. *D562 Transformation by bathing. C949.2 Baldness from breaking tabu. K2382.1 Bird plucks another bird's feathers out.* You may hear Maha Bounyok Saensouthone telling this story in Lao at http://www.seasite.niu.edu/lao/.

Part 6: Riddle Tales

Nine Bamboo Clumps. Told by Phra Wiangsamai, Vientiane, Laos. Collected and retold in English by Wajuppa Tossa.

The Serving Giant. Retold by Pha Sunantha Theerapanyophikkhu, Vientiane, Laos. Collected and retold in English by Wajuppa Tossa. *N813 Helpful genie. R181 Demon enclosed in bottle released. F403.2.2.4 Spirit in bottle (bag) as helper. K211 Devil cheated by imposing an impossible task. Types 1171-1199* list many such tasks. One child's answer to our story was *K717 Deception into bottle (vessel). Insects (or a spirit) having escaped from a bottle are told that they cannot return. They accept the challenge and go back into the bottle.*

The Father's Test. Retold by Phra Ajan Xaisomphone Phithiwan (Khen), Vientiane, Laos. Collected and retold in English by Wajuppa Tossa. This is *H200 Test of truth.* The test is sometimes executed by a king, sometimes by a father. It is related to *H588 Enigmatic counsels of father,* and to *H1023.1.1 Task: Hatching boiled eggs. Countertask: sowing cooked seed and harvesting the crop.*

Human's Age. Retold by Pha Sunantha Theerapanyophikku, Vientiane, Laos. Collected and retold in English by Wajuppa Tossa. *B841.2 Ages of animals (birds, fish) compared with age of human beings. W. Traits of character.*

Part 7: Ghost Stories

Phi Ya Wom: The Grandma Ghost Named Wom. From "Phi Ya Wom," by Somsaeng Kesawila, in *Hom Nithan Phuen Muen (Collected Lao Folktales)* (Vientiane: The Lao National Research Institute of Art and Culture, 1986), pp. 45–48. Retold by Wajuppa Tossa. *E253 Ghost tries to kill person for food.*

Phi Khongkoi: The Ghost Named Kongkoi. Told by Suphaphit Khantha, Mahasarakham, Thailand. Collected and retold in English by Wajuppa Tossa. Suphaphit was a second grader when she told this story at the 2000 Tellebration at Mahasarakham. Translated into English and retold here by Wajuppa Tossa. In a version of this tale told in Laos, a second man imitates the actions of the first and is killed by the ghost. *E474 Cohabitation of living person and ghost.*

Phi Khon Long: The Ghost Who Carried Her Own Coffin. Told by Bounyok Saensounthone, Vientiane, Laos. Collected and retold in English by Wajuppa Tossa.

E210 Dead lover's malevolent return; E443.2 Ghost laid by prayer; E281 Ghost haunts house.

Phi Khao Pun: The Noodle Seller Ghost. Told by Natthakan Photjanaphimon, Nongkhai, Thailand. Collected and retold in English by Wajuppa Tossa. The storyteller heard the story from her cousin, named Thanyawadee Seetonwong, who heard the story from her father or their grandfather. Natthakan was a student of Dr. Wajuppa Tossa. *Khao pun* is Thai rice noodles made from ground and fermented glutinous rice flour. Usually *khao pun* is eaten with fish condiment and fresh or steamed vegetables. *Xaleng* is a tricycle with the driver's seat beside the passenger seat plus a space for carrying things. *Z13.1 Tale-teller frightens listener: yells "Boo" at exciting point; E232 Return from dead to slay own murderer.*

Part 8: Tales of Magic and Elaborate Tales

Sang Sinxai. Retold by Kongdeuane Nettavong. Translated by Wajuppa Tossa. Kongdeaune heard this story and also read variants of the tale. *R154.1 Son rescues mother.* Stith Thompson cites variants of this from Ireland, India, and Buddhist tradition. *H911 Tasks assigned at suggestion of jealous rivals.*

Thao Khangkham, the Chameleon Prince. Told by Khamsing Wongsawang, National Libraries, Vientiane, Laos. Translated by Wajuppa Tossa. Khamsing had read the story in a palm leaf manuscript collected from one of the villages in Laos. In the old days people believed that writing down stories would be one way of making merit. These palm leaf manuscripts were preserved in families. Nowadays folks cannot read these, as they were written in an old Lao script. So a special project has been launched to preserve these. They are brought to the National Library from the villages, put onto microfiche, and then returned to the village with great ceremony and intent that the villagers will preserve these important texts. *B620 Animal suitor.* Stith Thompson lists many animal suitors, but none are chameleons. *C757.1 Tabu: Destroying animal skin of enchanted person too soon. D721.3 Disenchantment by destroying skin. H310 Suitor tests.* A suitor is put to severe tests by his prospective bride or father-in-law. This motif appears in many forms in tales from around the world. *H539.1 Suitor test: building causeway. (Irish)*

Thao Chet Hai. Retold by Wajuppa Tossa. "Thao Chet Hai" is retold in verse in the Lao National Library version published in 1971. The original manuscript was recovered at the Luang Phra Bang Library and was written in *Lao Dhamma* script. Normally, the *Dhamma* script was used to record religious or Buddhist texts, but this is an exception to the rule. There are other versions of the story as well. Another version in English could be found in Supaporn Vathanaprida's *Thai Tales: Folktales of Thailand* (Libraries Unlimited, 1994). An adapted version of the story is found in *Folktales and Story-*

telling by Wajuppa Tossa and Margaret Read MacDonald (Mahasarakham: Aphichaatkaanphim, 1986), pp. 92–98. This tale usually contains the motif *F601 Extraordinary companions. A group of men with extraordinary powers travel together.* But in this Lao version the heroes seem not to use their extraordinary powers. Probably a part of the story has been left out. *F612.1 Strong hero sent from home because of enormous appetite.* Stith Thompson gives variations on this motif from Brittany, Indonesia, Norway, and the Philippines. *F611.3.2 Hero's precocious strength. Has full strength when very young. F612.1 Strong hero sent from home because of enormous appetite.* This seems to be a common problem of strong heroes, as Stith Thompson cites here variants from France (Breton), The Netherlands, Norway, Indonesia, and the Philippines. *F531.3.10 Giants carry trees.* Irish and French Canadian variants. *F531.6.7.1 Giant possesses treasure.* Stith Thompson gives variants from Iceland, Norway, The Faroe Islands, Switzerland, and Styria. *N538.2 Treasure from defeated giant.* This reminds us also of the British tale of "Jack and the Beanstalk" (F54.1). An Isaan variant is found in Supaporn Vathanaprida's *Thai Tales: Folktales of Thailand* (Libraries Unlimited, 1994). Su's tale is taken from variants from Surin-Sisaket, Nakon Rachasima, and three other Isaan sources.

Seven Friends. Told by Somboon Thana-ouan, Mahasarakham, Thailand. Collected and retold in English by Wajuppa Tossa. Most of Somboon's tellings were in verse. Some of the original Lao is included here so the English audience can experience the poetic cadence. Stith Thompson gives one tale chain of repeated swallowings from a U.S. tale: *Z49.10 Lizard eats cricket, frog eats lizard, snake eats frog, eagle eats snake, man shoots eagle. K1718 Ogre overawed by hero's boasts about marvelous relatives.*

The Stingy Bird. Retold by Rerai Romyen from a version by Kamphon from Wapipathum School, Mahasarakham, Thailand. The phrase *khi thi* can be interpreted to mean "stingy." But the phrase also has overtones in Thai of other meanings. When a story is unbelievable a person could mutter, "*khi*," and *khi thi* can also mean "poop dropped closely together." The American storyteller David Holt retold this story as "The Freedom Bird" in *Ready-to-tell Tales* by David Holt and Bill Mooney (August House, 1994), pp. 220–22. *Z49.3 Bird indifferent to pain.* MacDonald & Sturm cite variants from India and the United States. MacDonald gives versions from Spain, Pakistan, India, and Uganda.

Part 9: Tales of Helpful Gods and Spirits

Nang Kaikaew: The Girl and the Precious Rooster. Retold by Kongdeuane Nettavong. Translated by Wajuppa Tossa. Ajan Kidaeng Phonekasoemsouk, a university professor, collected the story. He has published two Lao folktale collections. *B469.5 Helpful cock. B586 Animal gives treasure to man.* The tale is somewhat reminiscent of *D735.1 Beauty and the Beast. Disenchantment of animal.*

Kampha Khao To: The Orphan and the Rooster. Retold by Kongdeuane Nettavong. Translated by Wajuppa Tossa. *Q45 Hospitality rewarded.*

Namya Wiset: The Magic Water. Retold by Kongdeuane Nettavong. Translated by Wajuppa Tossa. Kongdeuane had heard this story. *D1338.1.1 Fountain of youth.* Stith Thompson gives sources from France, Ireland, Iceland, French Canadian, Greece, Japan, and Native American. The motif of amassing a large store of grains through the planting of a small quantity and repeating this over and over appears throughout Southeast Asia.

Yhaa Nuet Maew: The Magic Plant. Retold by Kongdeuane Nettavong. Translated by Wajuppa Tossa. Kongdeuane had heard this tale. *A1438 Origin of medicine. D1502.6 Magic object cures urinary disease.* Stith Thompson cites one Irish tale.

Part 10: Place Legends

The **Story of Vientiane.** Retold by Wajuppa Tossa. The story is adapted from *Nithan Souphasit (Moral Tales)* by Maha Chan Inthuphilaat (Vientiane: The Ministry of Education, n.d.). The stories in this collection have been prepared in looseleaf form for reading Lao lessons by Mr. Arthur Crisfield and his students from Southeast Asian Studies Summer Institute (SEASSI)1987. *F831 Extraordinary arrow. K710 Victim enticed into voluntary captivity or helplessness.*

The Casting of Pha Bang. Retold by Kongdeuane Nettavong. Translated by Wajuppa Tossa. Adapted from "The Casting of the Pra Bang," in *Legends of the Lao, a Compilation of Legends and other Folklore of the Lao People* by Xay Kaignavongsa and Hugh Fincher ([United States]: Geodata Systems, 1993), p. 63. *D1213 Magic Bell.*

The Legend of Phu Si. Retold by Chanpheng Singphet, Children's Culture Center, Luang Phabang. Collected and retold in English by Wajuppa Tossa. *A963 Mountains from stones (soil, sand) dropped or thrown.*

Phaya Sikhottabong. From *Sikhhottabong* by Duangkhai Luangphasi (Vientiane: Longphim haeng lat [The State Printing Press], 1990). Retold by Wajuppa Tossa. *F628.1.6 Strong hero fells maddened elephants. F610 Remarkably strong man.*

The Plain of Jars: Thong Haihin. Retold by Wajuppa Tossa. Dr. Wajuppa attempted to find more complete variants of this tale through interviews when traveling in the area of the Plain of Jars. She was unable to find anyone who had a more complete tale to tell. From the chronicles, however, we receive a more elaborate tale. See page 145.

The Forest Gibbons of Laos: Nang Zanee Khuan. Retold by Kongdeuane Nettavong. Translated by Wajuppa Tossa. Heard in her childhood. You may hear Kongdeuane Nettavong telling this tale in Lao at http://www.seasite.niu.edu/lao/. *T676 Childless couple adopt animal as substitute for child.*

Phu Pha Phu Nang: Prince Mountain and Princess Mountain. Retold by Kongdeuane Nettavong. Translated by Wajuppa Tossa. A folktale known to everyone in Luang Phabang. Abandoned children are rampant in folklore. Stith Thompson assigns a large swath to them, *S300-S399. B411.1 Helpful bull.* Bulls tend to be helpful animals throughout folk literature. Stith Thompson cites tales from Sweden, Ireland, France (Breton), Native American (Wyandot), and Missouri-French. *K987 Uriah letter. Man carries written order for his own execution. K511 Uriah letter changed.* This is another common folktale motif. Stith Thompson cites sources from French, Iceland, Germany, Greece, India, Japan, Africa, plus Jewish and Buddhist variants. *D672 Obstacle flight. Fugitives throw objects behind them which magically become obstacles in pursuer's path.* Stith Thompson cites sources of this popular motif from England, Scotland, Ireland, France (Breton), Switzerland, Iceland, Hungary, French Canadian, Jewish, India, Korea, Japan, Indonesia, the Philippines, the Marquesas, Native American (Yuchi), South American Indian (Mundurucú, Carajá , Ceiuci), Eskimo, Jamaica, and Africa (Basuto, Mpongwe, Kaffir). *A962.1 Mountain from part of deity's (hero's) body.*

Part 11: Origin Myths of the Lao People

The Great Gourd of Heaven: All Humanity from the Same Place. Retold by Wajuppa Tossa. *The Great Gourd of Heaven: A Selection of the Folk-tales and Stories of Laos* by Somvavanh Phanmatha. Collected by Roisin O. Boyle and Thavisack Phanmathanh (Vientiane: Vannasin Magazine, The Ministry of Information and Culture, 1992), pp. 1–3. *A1236.2 Tribes emerge from melon.* Stith Thompson cites one Lao variant. *F815.7.2 Gigantic vine.*

Khoun Bulom. Retold in English by Wajuppa Tossa. Information for this story comes from: The Literature Department, Ministry of Education, *Phuen Khun Boromrajathirat Sabab Buhan Tae (The Myth of Lord Boromrajathirat, the Truly Ancient Version)* (Vientiane: The Literature Department, Ministry of Education, 1967), pp. 44–48 and 66–147. And from a retelling by Sila Viravongs and Nuan Suthepsakda. *A1236.2 Tribes emerge from melon.* Jaruwan Thammawat, *Lae lod Phongsawadan Lao [Glimpses at the Lao Historical Chronicles]* (Mahasarakham: Mahasarakham University, n.d.); Souneth Phothisane, "The Nidan Khun Bulom: Annotated Translation and Analysis" (Ph.D. dissertation, University of Queensland, Australia, 1996), OCLC 40872003.

Khua Khao Kaad: The Giant Creeper. From *Kheu Khao Kaad* by Souban Luanglahd (Vientiane: Children's Cultural Center, with Japan-Lao Children Development Project, 1999). Retold by Wajuppa Tossa. Souban is director of the Children's Cultural Center of Laos. He has published several Lao folktales in Vientiane. *F815.7.2 Gigantic vine. A1236.2 Tribes emerge from melon.*

The Four Marvelous Brothers: A Folktale of the Lao Phuan People. Retold by Kongdeuane Nettavong. Translated by Wajuppa Tossa. Also in picture book format, *Four Marvelous Brothers* by Kongdeuane Nettavong. Illustrated by Nouannipha Mokham (Vientiane: National Library of Laos, 2000). *T543 Birth from plant. N827 Child as helper. Q192 Child given as reward for prayer. T548.1 Child born in answer to prayer. T549.1 Vegetable comes to life at woman's prayer. N831.1 Mysterious housekeeper.* The source of the mysterious helper varies, but such stories are told throughout the world. Stith Thompson cites tales of mysterious helpers from France (Breton), Missouri, Spain, Italy, India, China, Korea, Indonesia, the Philippines, Melanesia, New Britain, Eskimo, Native American, South American Indian, Surinam, and Africa (Ekoi, Congo, Basuto, Kaffir, Zulu). MacDonald cites sources from China, Ceylon, Italy, Russia, Nepal, and Greece. MacDonald & Sturm cite sources from Kenya (Luo) and Mexico. You may hear Kongdeuane Nettavong telling this tale in Lao at http://www.seasite.niu.edu/lao.

The Origin of the Mekong River. Retold by Wajuppa Tossa. This tale appears within the larger folk epic of Phadaeng Nang Ai, which Ajan Wajuppa has published in English. *Phadaeng Nang Ai* (Bucknell University Press, 1990). See note for "Phadaeng Nang Ai" below. *A930.1.1 Snake as creator of river. B91.1 Naga. B244.2 Naga King.*

Part 12: Folk Epics

Phya Khankhaak, The Toad King. Transcription of palm leaf manuscript by Phra Ariyanuwat Khemajari. Retold by Wajuppa Tossa from her English language epic, *Phya Khankhaak, the Toad King: A Translation of an Isan Fertility Myth in Verse* (Lewisburg, PA: Bucknell University Press, 1996). For a simpler version for easy storytelling, see "Phya Khankhaak, the Toad Prince," in *Five Minute Tales* by Margaret Read MacDonald (August House, 2007), pp. 27–30. For a similar tale from Burma, see "Little Thumb Conquers the Sun," in *Oryx Multicultural Folktale Series: Tom Thumb* by Margaret Read MacDonald (Oryx, 1993), pp. 102–9. This tale has some similarity to *Z52 Bird avenges mate. Arms self and proclaims war with king,* in which many helpers are enlisted to accompany the bird to threaten the king into submission. *D395 Frog transformed to person. B641.1.2 Marriage to person in frog form.* This story is told at the time of the *bun bangfai* rocket ceremony in Isaan and explains the reason for the festival.

Phadaeng Nang Ai. Transcription of palm leaf manuscript by Phra Ariyanuwat Khemajari. Retold by Wajuppa Tossa from *Phadaeng Nang Ai: A Translation of an Thai/Isan Folk Epic in Verse* (Lewisburg, PA: Bucknell University Press, 1990). *A934 Various origins of rivers. A930.1.1 Snake as creator of river. B91.1 Naga. B244.2 Naga King.* This story is told at the time of the *bun bangfai* rocket ceremony in Isaan.

Thao Hung Thao Cheuang. From *Thao Hung Thao Cheuang* by Doungdeuane (Viravongs) Bounyavong, Vientiane. Retold by Wajuppa Tossa. (Sources: *"Naewkkhid lae udomkhati nai mahakab Thao Hung Thao Cheuang,"* by Doungdeuane Viravongs Bounyavong, in *Thao Hung Thao Cheuang, Weeraburut Song Phang Kong [The Hero of the Two Sides of the Mekong River Banks]* (Bangkok: Phikkhanet Printing Center, 1995), pp. 182–253; "Luang Thao Hung Thao Cheuang" by Sila Viravongs, in *Payot khong wannakhadee [The Benefits of Literature]* (Vientiane: Phainam Kanphim, 1996), pp. 65–102; "Thao Hung Thao Cheuang" by Sila Viravongs, in *Thao Hung Kun Cheuang, Weeraburut Song Phang Khong [The Hero of the Two Sides of the Mekong River Banks]* (Bangkok: Phikkanet Printing Center, 1995), pp. 96–116; *Thao Hung Thao Cheuang Epic: Adaptation into Modern Prose,* by Sila Viravongs. Adapted and annotated by Doungdeuane Viravongs Bounyavong and others (Vientiane: The National Library of Laos, 2000). Muang Suajjntan is present-day Chiangrai, Thailand.)

GLOSSARY

Abbot: head of the temple

Ajan: teacher

Areca nut: tree nut that is chewed with betel leaf, lime, and other ingredients

Bael fruit: smooth, woody-skinned fruit about 5 to 15 centimeters in diameter

Betel leaf: tree leaf used to wrap areca nuts for chewing

Boon (*bun*): merit. When accumulated, merit helps one move on to a higher plane of existence in the next rebirth. Merit can be acquired by doing good works, contributing to the temple, or feeding the monks. Merit can also be made for the souls of deceased relatives.

Boun Phawet: Buddhist ritual celebrating the last rebirth of the Lord Buddha before he became Gautama. In that life he was reborn as Prince Wetsandon.

Brahman (Brahmin): holy man. In Laos called *mo phon* (blessing specialist). This is a respected ceremonial leader. In the stories imported from India, however, "brahman" refers to a priestly class.

Buddhaphisek: ceremony for the casting of a Buddha image

Buddhist Lent: religious season, from the full moon of the eighth lunar month to the full moon of the tenth lunar month

Devata (*devada*): celestial being in both Buddhist and animistic cosmology. *See also Thewada*

Dhamma (*Dharma*): religious scriptures.

Dhamma **script:** language used to write down religious scriptures

Garuda: mythical winged creature

Hanuman: Monkey King who aided Sita and Rama in their epic tale

Himmaphan Forest: sacred forest in Indian epics

Indra: Phra Indra is a high god in the sixth realm of the heavens. In Thai Buddhist cosmology there are thirty-one realms, and the first six are sensual. Beginning from the seventh realm, the beings have less and less attachment to worldly feelings. Buddha is in the seventh realm.

Ikat: method of weaving that requires that threads be tied together in certain patterns for dying *before* weaving begins. Thus the weaving must be done very carefully, in order to align the pre-dyed designs exactly as the weaving progresses.

Jātaka **tales**: stories of the rebirths of the Lord Buddha. He was reborn many times, and in each life his incarnation did something benevolent.

Kaxoum **bird**: lesser adjutant stork

Khaen: instrument made of several bamboo pipes fastened together. A wooden mouthpiece is fastened, holding the pipes together, and metal reeds in the mouthpiece vibrate as the khaen is blown, creating a loud, nasal sound.

Khao pun: rice noodles

Khun: sir or madame

Kuti: sleeping quarters of monks.

Maak khing: cannonball fruit

Maeng Nguan: the singing cricket

Mo lam: folk opera. *Mo lam* troupes tour the countryside

Muang: city

Naga: mythical dragonlike snake. Sometimes *naga* refers to a large snake like a huge magical cobra; at other times it refers to a more dragonlike creature.

Nang: madame

Nirvana: ultimate plane of being, actually a state of nonbeing

Novice: person studying for the monkhood. In Lao tradition persons may enter a *wat* as a novice for short periods of time in order to gain merit.

Pali: script from India. Used for sacred manuscripts.

Panya: wisdom

Pha: *See* Phya

Phakhawma: piece of cloth wrapped around the waist, worn by men. Also useful to carry things, as a towel, and for any other use a cloth might have.

Phi (pi): ghost, or spirit of the deceased; can be friendly or malevolent

Phu (**pu**): mountain

Phya: lord

Phya In: supreme god of the heavens. *See also* Indra

Pra: *See* Phya

Rishi (**risi**): hermit, usually living deep in the forest

Sangkha (Sangha): brotherhood of monks of the Buddhist faith

Sida (Sita): wife of Rama. Their Indian epic is retold throughout Southeast Asia.

Thao: title for a man in an old Thai/Lao community

Thaen: Creator of natural phenomena; the rain god. Phya Thaen is a ruler in heaven.

Thewada (Thevada): magical beings, often found living in trees, able to grant wishes. Thevada also attend on Phya Thaen in heaven. *See also Devata*

Thid: title for a man who has been ordained as a monk at some time in his life

Wai: position for prayer or greeting. Hands are placed palm to palm, fingers pointing up, held at chest level. A sign of respect.

Wat: Buddhist temple and its grounds

Wetsandon (Vessandon): the Buddha's last incarnation before becoming the BuddhaWetsandon. The story of Phra Wetsandon is a particularly holy legend.

Xadouk: *See Jātaka*

Xaleng: A motorcycle-engine-powered three-wheeled vehicle.

Xiang Miang: name of a trickster character

Ya: grandmother

Yak: giant; *see* photograph in color section.

INDEX

Sikaew, 154
Sikhottabong, 4, 120
Sila, 6
Silver, father and mother of, 92
Silver working, 6
Simpsong Panna, 4
Singing animals approach heaven,
     148–149
Singing cricket, 51–52
Singman Village, 125
Singmou, 6
Singphet, Changpheng ix, 118
Singsali, 6
Sinxai, 89–90
Sipsong Cuthai, 4
Sita, 118
Sithom, 157
Skin, of chameleon burnt, 92
Sleeping, 67
Snail race, 28–29
Snakes, 49
Snake biting tail game, 174
     origin of, 78
Somphone, Sombath ix
Somsa, Suched ix
Son, born, 23
Sons, magical, 138–140
Sopha, Sivilay, x, 18, 49
Souai, 6
Soutto, 152–153, 155
Soutto, 152. *See also* Souttoranark
Souttoranark, 141
Souvan, 152. *See also* Souvanranark
Souvanranark , 141
Soy beans, 5
Spelling, x
Spring roll recipe, 171
Squash, 50, 138
Squirrel, 49
     white, 154–155
Sri Lanka, 116
Sticky rice, 1, 5, 120, 168
Stingy bird, 100–101
Stork, origin bald head, 58–60
Storytelling, teaching xii

Strength, source of, 121
Studying, 67
Suantan, 156–157
Suriyawongsathammathirat, Phachao, 4
Suwwanakhomkham, 4
Swallows, salted, 5
Swan
     carries man, 18
     golden, 17
     judges, 59
     white, 18–19
Swans, 11–13

Tai daeng, 5
Tai dam, 5
Tai Eing, 159
Tai Kwang, 134
Tai Lee, 134
Tai Loeng, 134
Tai Lom, 134
Tai neua, 5
Tai phuan, 5
Tai-Lao language groups, 5
Tall tales to intimidate ogress, 97–98
Talum, 59
Tam maak hung, 170
Ta-oi, 6
Target game, 175
Taro, 6
Tasks must be assigned, 65–67
Temple. *See Wat*
Temptation, 99
Thaen, 128. *See also* Phya Thaen
     thank for food, 133–134
Thaen Kingdom, 159
Thaen Lo, 159
Thaenfeuang, 159
Thaenkokay, 159
Thaenlee, 159
Thaenlom, 159
Thaenmeng, 159
Thaenmok, 159
Thaenna, Khambao, x, 45
Thaensong, 159
Thaenthao, 159

ABOUT THE EDITOR
AND AUTHORS

Margaret Read MacDonald, editor, was a Fulbright Scholar to the University of Mahasarakham in 2005–2006, working under the direction of Dr. Wajuppa Tossa. She has returned to Thailand many times and has often hosted Dr. Wajuppa and her storytelling students on Guemes Island, Washington. In 2006 she toured in Laos with Dr. Wajuppa and her storytelling troupe. MacDonald has worked with storytellers from various countries to prepare folktale collections for the Libraries Unlimited World Folklore Series: *Indonesian Folktales* by Murti Bunanta, *From the Winds of Manguito*: *Cuban Folklore* by Elvia Pérez, *Brazilian Folktales* by Livia de Almeida, and *Thai Tales* by Supaporn Vathanaprida. She is currently working with Paula Martín of Argentina on *Pacha Mama* and with various Malaysian tellers on *Malaysian Folktales*.

Kongdeuane Nettavong is the director of the Lao National Library in Vientiane, Laos. She received her master's degree in archives in 1974 from Saint Cloud, Paris, France. Her work in the preservation of Lao cultural heritage is extensive and ongoing. She served several terms as a subcommittee member for culture and education for ASEAN and ACCU-UNESCO. She heads the Preservation of Lao Palm-leaf Manuscripts Program (Lao-German Cooperation Project) and the National Reading Promotion Project through Puppet Theater, and is a permanent consultant to the Lao Children's Cultural Center and Children's Home for Culture. Her publications include a picture book, *Four Marvelous Brothers* (2002); *Fifty Lao Classic Folktales Related to Herbal Medicine* (2007); *Khaen and the Melodies of Khaen* (2007); and *Lao Intangible Culture: The Sukhwan Ceremony*. Her research topics include Lao herbal folk medicine, Lao folktales, and Lao intangible culture. She is also a storyteller, musician, and writer.

Wajuppa Tossa (l), Kongdeuane Nettavong (r)

Dr. Wajuppa Tossa is an associate professor of English and American Literature at Mahasarakham University, Thailand. Since graduation from Drew University (New Jersey) with a Ph.D. in English and American literature, she has published two translations of Isaan folk epics, *Phadaeng Nang Ai* (1990) and *Phya Khankhaak, the Toad King* (1996). With support from the Fulbright, John F. Kennedy of Thailand, and J. H. Thompson Foundations, she has been working on the preservation of Thai/Lao folktales and storytelling since 1995. This work is described in "Engendering Cultural Pride Through Storytelling," co-authored with Margaret Read MacDonald (in *The Arts, Education, and Social Change: Little Signs of Hope*. Lesley University Series in Arts and Education, vol. 9. New York: Peter Lang Publishing, 2005). Dr. Wajuppa Tossa is also a storyteller, touring and giving storytelling performances in and outside of Thailand. She has performed in Malaysia, Laos, Singapore, Hong Kong, China, Australia, The Netherlands, and the United States. She delights her audiences, students, and workshop participants by sharing her love of folktales and the art of storytelling in her presentations. She is particularly keen on the use of folktales and storytelling in her career as a teacher and facilitator.

Recent Titles in the
World Folklore Series

Additional titles in this series can be found at www.lu.com